# Making the Library Accessible for All

# PRACTICAL GUIDES FOR LIBRARIANS

## About the Series

This innovative series written and edited for librarians by librarians provides authoritative, practical information and guidance on a wide spectrum of library processes and operations.

Books in the series are focused, describing practical and innovative solutions to a problem facing today's librarian and delivering step-by-step guidance for planning, creating, implementing, managing, and evaluating a wide range of services and programs.

The books are aimed at beginning and intermediate librarians needing basic instruction/guidance in a specific subject and at experienced librarians who need to gain knowledge in a new area or guidance in implementing a new program/service.

## About the Series Editor

The **Practical Guides for Librarians** series was conceived by and is edited by M. Sandra Wood, MLS, MBA, AHIP, FMLA, Librarian Emerita, Penn State University Libraries.

M. Sandra Wood was a librarian at the George T. Harrell Library, The Milton S. Hershey Medical Center, College of Medicine, Pennsylvania State University, Hershey, PA, for over 35 years, specializing in reference, educational, and database services. Ms. Wood worked for several years as a Development Editor for Neal-Schuman Publishers.

Ms. Wood received a MLS from Indiana University and a MBA from the University of Maryland. She is a Fellow of the Medical Library Association and served as a member of MLA's Board of Directors from 1991 to 1995. Ms. Wood is founding and current editor of *Medical Reference Services Quarterly*, now in its 35th volume. She also was founding editor of the *Journal of Consumer Health on the Internet* and the *Journal of Electronic Resources in Medical Libraries* and served as editor/co-editor of both journals through 2011.

## Titles in the Series

1. *How to Teach: A Practical Guide for Librarians* by Beverley E. Crane.

2. *Implementing an Inclusive Staffing Model for Today's Reference Services* by Julia K. Nims, Paula Storm, and Robert Stevens.

3. *Managing Digital Audiovisual Resources: A Practical Guide for Librarians* by Matthew C. Mariner.

4. *Outsourcing Technology: A Practical Guide for Librarians* by Robin Hastings.

5. *Making the Library Accessible for All: A Practical Guide for Librarians* by Jane Vincent.

# Making the Library Accessible for All

## A Practical Guide for Librarians

## Jane Vincent

PRACTICAL GUIDES FOR LIBRARIANS, NO. 5

ROWMAN & LITTLEFIELD
*Lanham • Boulder • New York • Toronto • Plymouth, UK*

Published by Rowman & Littlefield
4501 Forbes Boulevard, Suite 200, Lanham, Maryland 20706
www.rowman.com

10 Thornbury Road, Plymouth PL6 7PP, United Kingdom

British Library Cataloguing in Publication Information Available

**Library of Congress Cataloging-in-Publication Data**

Vincent, Jane.
  Making the library accessible for all : a practical guide for librarians / Jane Vincent.
      pages cm. — (Practical guides for librarians ; no. 5)
  Includes bibliographical references and index.
  ISBN 978-0-8108-9146-3 (pbk. : alk. paper) — ISBN 978-0-8108-9147-0 (ebook)  1.
Libraries and people with disabilities. 2.  Libraries and people with disabilities—United States.
3.  Self-help devices for people with disabilities. 4.  Assistive computer technology. I. Title.
  Z711.92.H3V57 2014
  027.6′63—dc23                                                                          2013047558

∞™ The paper used in this publication meets the minimum requirements of American
National Standard for Information Sciences—Permanence of Paper for Printed Library
Materials, ANSI/NISO Z39.48-1992. Printed in the United States of America

*For the students of the University of Michigan School of Information*

*You are the shining future of our profession*

# Contents

# List of Illustrations

## ⊚ Figures

# Preface

Your library needs and wants to attract more patrons with disabilities.

Odds are, you bought or borrowed this book because you were concerned about meeting legal requirements or perhaps because you have already seen some people with obvious disabilities come to your library and you want to provide them with excellent service. It is probably not yet second nature for you to think about the benefits of providing an environment so that your library can actively attract many patrons with disabilities. These benefits may include, but not be limited to, the following.

## Fresh Perspectives

Every library can use a new infusion of patrons. Are you having problems attracting enough attendees to the computer training classes that your library board president insists you conduct? Local people with disabilities may not have thought to seek training at their library and may welcome the opportunity. Are people complaining that your programming is getting repetitive? Asking disabled patrons for suggestions on what films to show at a disability film festival and having them lead discussions afterward may expose your community to novel ideas and perspectives. Are you lobbying to your city council for a new bus stop in front of the library? Collecting affidavits of support from wheelchair users will likely be very helpful.

## Impetus

In all likelihood, most libraries have at least one thing that many patrons, perhaps even staff, find annoying but not enough to formally complain—say, a large planter that people keep walking into. As you start to review your library for compliance with the Americans with Disabilities Act (ADA) requirements for architecture (see chapter 4), you realize that the planter protrudes more than 4 inches into the walkway and is therefore out of compliance. Planter gets moved. Your library immediately becomes more ADA compliant. Fewer shins are bruised. Everyone is happy.

# ⊚ Enthusiasm

The most important thing to remember is that patrons are showing up not because they have a disability but because you have a library, and libraries have much to offer. If patrons find your library to be accessible on top of everything else that it provides, they are likely to spread the word among their peers and colleagues, resulting in an increased stream of satisfied patrons and an enhancement to the library's positive reputation.

It is easy to assume, for example, that blind people are not interested in coming to public libraries. Computer accessibility expert and library enthusiast Marc Sutton (2013, personal correspondence) provides an explanation to the contrary:

> I am a blind person who has loved reading since I picked up my first braille book at the age of 5. It has always been a challenge to find reading material in a nonprint format. There are a variety of sources for accessible reading material such as the National Library Service for the Blind and Physically Handicapped, commercial audio and electronic book companies. However, their offerings fall far short of being able to provide access to even a small percentage of published print materials. Public libraries can provide an invaluable resource for blind patrons by helping streamline all of these sources, providing accessible reference materials, and promoting the accessibility of online sources of reading material.
>
> Another important service is the provision of accessible computers which enable patrons to look up and check out materials on the library catalog, and to research, and perform other related tasks. There are many books and magazines available through online library databases that would otherwise not be accessible to print-impaired persons. Often, a patron just needs a little help finding these items and then a whole new world of knowledge opens up.
>
> Historically, blind and visually impaired persons have not come close to utilizing the many resources and materials that are available in public libraries. Librarians can contribute to significantly changing this relationship.

Once you make a commitment to increasing your library's accessibility, there will be many "how to" questions. How can we accommodate Deaf patrons in our lecture series? How can a blind person use a computer? How do I communicate respectfully with someone who does not speak? How can an Autistic child successfully participate in story time? *Making the Library Accessible for All* is designed to provide the answer to a broad range of these questions.

# ⊚ Who Needs Accessibility?

Libraries have often adopted the phrase "ADA patrons," with the potential implication that only people covered by the ADA require accommodations. While libraries do have responsibilities for ADA compliance, many people would not be covered by the ADA, but they would still need and benefit from accessible equipment, interactions, and environments. It is probably more useful to think in terms of the full range of patrons and staff who might find given designs, policies, or practices to be accommodations or impediments. For example, let's say that you are planning to select and install new automated checkout machines. There are many factors to consider that may affect who are able to use them effectively, including the following:

- Is at least one machine mounted low enough so that wheelchair users, short-statured people, and kids can access it?
- Is the display easy to see for people with low vision, including people with natural aging-related vision changes?
- Will the on-screen prompts be easy to understand by people with cognitive disabilities and for people using the machine for the first time? Is there an option to have the prompts spoken, to benefit not only blind people but also people who have learning disabilities or those for whom English is a second language?
- Will it be easy for people with dexterity disabilities to scan the bar code? Is scanning accurate enough so that people with low patience thresholds—whether related to an emotional disability or not—will be satisfied with the speed of the transaction?

The best way to anticipate and address these factors will be to get input from as many patrons as possible, including those with disabilities. Throughout this book, there are references to consulting with "accessibility resource people" on key issues to ensure that there is input from authorities on disability—ideally, those who experience it directly, as well as their supporters—to address accessibility up-front rather than as an afterthought.

## Library Responsibilities for Accessibility

Public libraries are likely to be considered responsible under Title II of the ADA, which covers state and municipal services. Determination of whether an organization is a "public entity" and therefore subject to Title II coverage includes the following:

1) Whether the entity is operated with public funds;
2) Whether the entity's employees are considered government employees;
3) Whether the entity receives significant assistance from the government by provision of property or equipment; and
4) Whether the entity is governed by an independent board selected by members of a private organization or a board elected by the voters or appointed by elected officials. (Department of Justice 2013a)

Most other libraries are likely covered by Title III, which addresses accessibility of "places of public accommodation"; libraries are specifically mentioned in the definition of this phrase (Department of Justice 2013b). The ADA does not cover libraries in private settings, such as libraries that are part of a residential community, a religious organization, or a private club. However, there is nothing that would prevent these entities from choosing to meet or exceed ADA guidelines.

A number of other factors may affect compliance requirements, such as proximity of library branches to one another and the year that the library building was constructed. There may also be other applicable legislation, such as state or municipal requirements. This book mentions several instances where consultation with library legal counsel is recommended to ensure that both the letter and the spirit of the law are addressed.

Beyond legal responsibilities, there are professional responsibilities that impel libraries to be usable by all patrons. The International Federation of Library Associations and Institutions published a "Code of Ethics for Librarians and Other Information Workers" in 2012 that includes several items directly relevant to accessibility, particularly the following:

- "In order to promote inclusion and eradicate discrimination, librarians and other information workers ensure that the right of accessing information is not denied and that equitable services are provided for everyone whatever their . . . physical or mental ability."
- "Librarians and other information workers organize and present content in a way that allows an autonomous user to find the information s/he needs. Librarians and other information workers help and support users in their information searching."
- "Librarians and other information workers offer services to increase reading skills."
- "Librarians and other information workers have a professional duty to advocate for exceptions and limitations to copyright restrictions for libraries."

## ⑥ Organization of This Book

*Making the Library Accessible for All: A Practical Guide for Librarians* consists of eight chapters, plus a glossary. It is designed to cover the most universal library features that may provide barriers to accessibility, while offering ideas on how to address situations unique to your library and its patrons.

Chapter 1, "What Is Accessibility?" gives you a starting place to assess your library's particular needs, whether addressed proactively through seeking input from current and potential accessibility resource people or through dealing with requests as they come up. It also provides an overview of when accessibility needs to be addressed through use of policies, including the importance of involving all staff members in your accessibility approach.

Communication between librarians and patrons is important in all cases, but there may be specific considerations involved when a patron has one or more disabilities. Chapter 2, "Communication Accessibility," covers etiquette so that staff and patrons will feel at ease, as well as technical considerations that facilitate communication with a broad contingent of patrons.

While most libraries still provide printed books and magazines, they may also provide materials in a range of electronic formats, including e-books. Chapter 3, "Materials Accessibility," focuses on barriers that each of these formats may provide and how they can be addressed. The chapter also discusses considerations for DVDs and other audio or multimedia formats.

Chapter 4, "Architectural and Environmental Accessibility," guides readers through the 2010 standards, the most recent specifications published by the federal government to address architectural barriers. It also goes beyond these standards to look at issues related to noise level, chemical sensitivity triggers, and other potential barriers in the library environment.

Modern libraries play an important role as community cultural centers, providing trainings, exhibits, and many types of events. To ensure that these are accessible to as many people as possible, chapter 5, "Training and Event Accessibility," looks at addressing issues throughout the event-planning process, from sending out the community invitation to holding the actual event. It also provides some suggestions for making virtual events such as webinars accessible.

Public transportation on the information highway is primarily provided by libraries, and an increasing variety of electronic devices—computers, tablets, e-readers—are provided for in-house use or even loan. Many of these devices need to be adapted to be accessible. Others have accessibility built in, but this may not be well documented. Chapter 6, "Technology Accessibility," discusses the features of these devices that may cause accessibility problems today as well as appropriate solutions, and it provides suggestions for keeping accessibility in mind as new products are released.

No matter how accessible an Internet-enabled device may be, users may still have problems if the website with which they are trying to use it has not been configured properly. Chapter 7, "Web Accessibility," covers ways to make sure that your library website is accessible; it also provides information that will be useful when applying your access standards to the selection of products from third-party vendors.

Finally, chapter 8, "The Accessible Library," provides tips on advocating for accessibility to your library administration and working with patrons when accessibility requests cannot be fulfilled. It ends with suggestions for incorporating broader accessibility awareness into the library field, through education, opportunities for librarians with disabilities, and increased awareness of disability culture.

The immediate purpose of this book is to provide detailed information about legislation, guidelines, best practices, and other topics that can improve the accessibility of your library. If it truly succeeds, however, it will also raise awareness of the rewards of actively accommodating and therefore welcoming patrons with disabilities to your library to the point where it becomes a part of your organizational culture.

# References

Department of Justice. 2013a. "The Americans with Disabilities Act Title II Technical Assistance Manual Covering State and Local Government Programs and Services." http://www.ada.gov/taman2.html#II-1.2000.

———. 2013b. "Title III Highlights." http://www.ada.gov/t3hilght.htm.

International Federation of Library Associations and Institutions. 2012. "IFLA Code of Ethics for Librarians and Other Information Workers (Full Version)." http://www.ifla.org/news/ifla-code-of-ethics-for-librarians-and-other-information-workers-full-version.

# Acknowledgments

Sandy Wood and Charles Harmon made this easy, again.

Thanks to Art Durkee (http://www.arthurdurkee.net) and Diane Dew (http://dianedew.smugmug.com) for their pictorial assistance.

My colleagues at the University of Michigan give me reasons to smile every workday. Particular thanks to Anna Ercoli Schnitzer for her belief in me; Jack Bernard and Carole Dubritsky for their commitment to accessibility; Laura Patterson, Rich Wong, John Hufziger, and Judy Smutek for their support; and Scott Williams for his insight and humor. Kudos to the Office of Services for Students with Disabilities: Stuart Segal, Alfred Kellam, Dan Measel, Jill Rice, Mary Reilly, Maureen Candy, and Virginia Grubaugh. I also thank Amy Wang, Barb Binetti, Bill Wrobleski, Bob and Annette Fraser, Bob Sabourin, Carolyn Grawi, Clive D'Souza, Darlene Nichols, Deirdre Spencer, Donna Goodin, Els Nieuwenhuijsen, Gary Munce, Heidi Koester, Jim Bujaki, John Cady, John Gohsman, Jorge Toral, Joyojeet Pal, Judy Walker, Laura Shelp, Laurel Barnes, Lisa Bartlett, Lisa Clark, Lloyd Shelton, Margaret Leary, Mary Gohsman, Melanie Yergeau, Melissa Levine, Mike Stork, Nisha Erinjeri, Nyshourn Price, Pamela Fons, Patricia Anderson, Paul Barrow, Paul Guttman, Petra Kuppers, Rebecca Dunkle, Rita Girardi, Ruth Addis, Ryan Echlin, Ryan Vis, Sam Goodin, Stefanie Horvath, Steve Griffes, Steve Sarrica, Svetla Sytch, Tamara McKay, and Will Winston. Jim Knox and Doug Thompson are always looking over my shoulder.

Deep thanks to my chapter reviewers: Debi Griffith, Betty Lutton Luscher, Ken Petri, Meriah Nichols, Carole Dubritsky, Alan Bern, John Cady, Jim Tobias, Anna Schnitzer, and Scott Williams. The book is enriched by individuals from inside and outside the library field who have kindly either given reprint permission or provided new material: Marc Sutton, Gina Worsham, Carrie Brooks, Alan Bern, Meriah Nichols, and Dey Alexander.

Roberta (and Winnie) Knox and Lisa Bednarz made my move back to Ann Arbor practical; Paul Armstrong and Bruce Oshaben made it fun. Jim Lillie is the best chef ever. Doug Day was my vigilant high school English teacher. Gregg Vanderheiden, Jim Tobias, and Rhea Rubin have long been supportive and patient mentors. The Hoy family is wonderful. In memoriam, Cheryl Marie Wade, Frank Moore, and Nick Feldman.

Finally, I am indebted to Madeleine, who provided just the right amount of distraction while saving me from spiders and catnip mice. *Mrrow*, Maddie.

# Introduction

This book is intended as a collection and, where helpful, interpretation of the most useful resources on accessibility in libraries and similar public areas that are currently available. At this time, the Americans with Disabilities Act provides highly specific guidance only on architecture (chapter 4) and is expected to soon release guidelines on web accessibility (chapter 7). As the chapters indicate, even these do not provide a full picture of what may be necessary. The act's language, as related to other areas where libraries may need to provide access, can be vague, and successful implementation is therefore reliant on combining an awareness of best practices and the needs of your specific library.

Keep in mind that your aim, like the aim of legislation, is to provide an equitable experience for your patrons with and without disabilities. If creative interpretations result in something that provides a higher level of genuine accessibility, even your legal counsel is likely to find that ultimately preferable to a strict but illogical adherence to the letter of the law or best practice. This book repeatedly encourages you to communicate with disabled people as experts on their needs; also keep in mind that you and your colleagues are the experts on your library. The process of implementing accommodation should therefore stem from a collaboration among people with two kinds of expertise, which increases the potential for success.

While this book primarily draws on information from the library world, it uses examples from other milieus, such as business. If you are looking for guidance on topics not covered here, check your shelves or your favorite search engine for ideas from any type of resource that may help provide answers or generate questions for additional exploration.

# List of Acronyms and Abbreviations

ADA:        Americans with Disabilities Act
CART:       computer-assisted real-time translation
CCTV:       closed-circuit television
LGBT:       lesbian/gay/bisexual/trans
OCR:        optical character recognition
OTC:        Oral Transliteration Certificate
POUR:       perceivable, operable, understandable, robust
TTY:        text telephone
VPAT:       Voluntary Product Accessibility Template
VRI:        video remote interpreting
VRS:        video relay services
WCAG:       Web Content Accessibility Guidelines
W3C:        World Wide Web Consortium

# What Is Accessibility?

A barrier can be anything that limits a person's movement or communications, or an attitude that discourages participation. If you are a wheelchair or scooter user and there are curbs with no ramps or steps, this is an obstruction and therefore a barrier to mobility. If you require someone to help you find something because you are blind and staff are not available to assist, this is a barrier to service. (Murphy 2007, 100)

AS MENTIONED IN THE INTRODUCTION, libraries have both a legal and a professional obligation to provide an accessible environment. But what does accessibility mean? The answer is as idiosyncratic as your patrons:

- It might mean that someone who cannot see or hold a book can savor that hot new novel in a format other than print.
- It might mean that a Deaf patron has access to videos with captions so that she can decide for herself whether Jim Carrey really is funny.
- It might mean that someone is able to maneuver his wheelchair easily and discreetly out of an event room to take a bathroom break while missing as little of a really interesting lecture as possible.
- It might mean that a middle-aged patron can do research on a computer without having to constantly squint.
- It might mean that a child with autism can get some extra time to interact with a librarian during story hour, or it might mean that a child with autism can avoid having to interact with anyone.

In short, accessibility really means that disabled patrons have an opportunity to focus on taking advantage of what the library has to offer, instead of focusing on dealing with the types of barriers that Tish Murphy lists in the quotation. It also means that both you and your patrons will benefit from communication about accommodations that are needed or preferred, rather than having librarians try to guess what would be best.

Legal mandates can be tremendously helpful in determining how to deal with some types of barriers, and these are cited where appropriate throughout this book. However, legislation goes only so far in addressing all the ways in which a particular library can meet the needs of its distinctive user base. To complete the picture, it is necessary to do some investigation into local needs and to create a consistent level of service. The former can be achieved through active and responsive outreach; the latter can be achieved by establishing policies and procedures and by creating a staff training program to communicate them.

# Legal Concepts: Reasonable Modifications and Fundamental Alterations

The technical assistance manuals for Title II and Title III of the Americans with Disabilities Act (ADA) contain statements about reasonable modifications and fundamental alterations. Both manuals provide examples of what these concepts may mean. The gist is that changes to services and other offerings should be made so that they can be provided equitably to people with and without disabilities, unless there would be "a change that is so significant that it alters the essential nature of the goods, services, facilities, privileges, advantages, or accommodations offered" (ADA.gov 2005).

> Title II: A public entity must reasonably modify its policies, practices, or procedures to avoid discrimination. If the public entity can demonstrate, however, that the modifications would fundamentally alter the nature of its service, program, or activity, it is not required to make the modification. (Department of Justice 1993a)

> Title III: A public accommodation must reasonably modify its policies, practices, or procedures to avoid discrimination. If the public accommodation can demonstrate, however, that a modification would fundamentally alter the nature of the goods, services, facilities, privileges, advantages, or accommodations it provides, it is not required to make the modification. (Department of Justice 1993b)

Part of what this means is that if the library offers a service—story time, word-processing software, public bathrooms—it is required to make this service accessible to people with disabilities. If it does not provide this service, it is not required to start providing it. Exorbitant cost and addressing safety concerns (e.g., a service dog that threatens other patrons, destroys furniture, or is not housebroken) may also legally override reasonable modification. Make sure that you are in close communication with the library's legal counsel before deciding that a nonemergency request should be denied because it represents a fundamental alteration.

Understandably, there may occasionally be differences in opinion between patrons and library personnel regarding what is "reasonable." While this book attempts to list the areas within a library where the need for accommodations may be expected, it cannot cover every possible accommodation situation. Chapter 8 covers strategies for discussing unusual or hard-to-implement requests with patrons.

There is no legal prohibition to a library going above and beyond what might be considered reasonable. If patrons are requesting a service or service modification that seems to exceed the legal requirements and if it makes sense for your library, go ahead with the implementation.

# ⊚ Active/Anticipatory Outreach: Accessibility Resource People

There is, perhaps, nothing more important than a focus group—or, better, an ongoing Advisory Group—to discuss accessibility issues at your library. You WILL get requests you cannot meet—and even off-base questions and requests—but the number of spot-on questions and requests AND unexpected, fantastic ideas far outweighs any negative outcomes. Do it! By the way, there is great community goodwill engendered by setting up a focus group and/or Advisory Group. (Alan Bern, Berkeley Public Library, personal communication, 2013)

Talking to people about the accommodations that they need and want is about empowerment and legal compliance, but it is also about pragmatics. It is difficult, if not impossible, for someone who does not use a wheelchair daily to anticipate the types of accommodations that would facilitate full access to your library, or for someone who does not have attention-deficit disorder to gauge what would make a person with it feel comfortable in a training class. Toward this end, you will want to put together a list of accessibility resource people—individuals who can provide input on local accessibility issues, from disability-specific language used in your area (see chapter 2) to assistive computer technologies that local individuals use (see chapter 6) to references to sign language interpreters and other professionals who serve your area (see chapter 5).

Ideally, the majority of these resources should be people with disabilities themselves. To recruit people with disabilities and to find other individuals who might have information to share, use your standard library communication channels—newsletter, posters, radio, and so on. Since people with disabilities will be part of any demographic, be sure to also notify any existing library groups, such as literacy initiatives. To ensure that you continue to get a broad picture of user needs and preferences, recruit new resource people on an ongoing basis.

In previous work (Vincent 2012, 9), I have recommended the following additional places to contact for recruitment of individuals with disabilities as well as other accessibility resource people:

- Local disability organizations
- Educational institutions
- Senior centers and other elder-focused resources
- Municipal government resources
- Hospitals and other medical resources

There are a number of ways that you might solicit input from these people:

- Focus groups
- Surveys
- Subject matter experts

## Focus Groups

Ongoing in-person focus groups are a powerful way for libraries to obtain input. If your library has not conducted focus groups before, Carter McNamara's web page "Basics of Conducting Focus Groups" and Rachel Flagg's "Focus Group Fundamentals for Government Programs" provide good guides to start with.

If you do hold in-person meetings, be sure to consult chapter 5, "Training and Event Accessibility," for information about making these meetings accessible. Depending on the questions that you plan to ask and your meeting accommodation strategies, you may decide to hold groups representing individual types of disabilities or groups representing a variety of disabilities.

## Surveys

Although "focus group" has usually implied that people meet in person, some people with disabilities may find it difficult to attend face-to-face meetings due to transportation issues, discomfort in social situations, or other factors. To reach a representative user sample, you will likely want to create a variety of ways to receive input, applying the information about materials accessibility provided in chapter 4. Ensure that respondents can submit input anonymously if they wish, through an online survey, a voice mailbox, and so forth. If you decide to do an online survey, SurveyMonkey is generally considered to be the most accessible service and permits generation of short surveys at no cost.

## Subject Matter Experts

As you make various connections, you will likely find people who have expertise in particular areas. Although it can be problematic to make generalizations based on one person's input, it can be very helpful to have "go-to" persons who can provide at least an initial response or give ideas for additional questions that need to be asked.

If particular questions come up that your local resource people cannot answer, try communicating with other librarians or search the Internet. Library conferences will often have at least one presentation related to accessibility (see chapter 8), and it is worth seeking these out or requesting materials from the presenters as additional resources.

# ◎ Handling Input

Throughout this book, there are references to questions that your accessibility resource people may be able to help answer. Appendix A provides a summary of these questions that can be used for your initial outreach.

Once you have received input, treat it as you would any information from community members. In particular, if you have heard from multiple people, look for trends that can be used in planning and practice. Use your communication channels to publicize your conclusions and provide information on how the library plans to respond.

Ideally, your relationship with your accessibility resource people will be ongoing, allowing you to bring up other questions as they arise. These partnerships may allow you to get quick feedback on some issues as well as open the door for other mutual benefits, such as resource sharing.

# ⊚ Responsive Outreach: The Reference Interview

The reference interview has always been an effective library tool for helping patrons find information. It is likely to prove equally useful for helping determine how best to accommodate patrons with disabilities when an accommodation is requested.

Iowa Library Services (2013) lists seven steps for a productive reference interview:

Step 1: Approachability

Step 2: Interest

Step 3: Listening

Step 4: Interviewing

Step 5: Searching

Step 6: Answering

Step 7: Follow-up

When you are talking with a patron about a requested accommodation, this is a good model to use. As illustrative examples, let's say that you are working with two patrons who have made requests:

- Mohammed, who uses a communication board (see chapter 2), has asked for brainstorming assistance so that his attendant can create a board specifically for use at the library.
- Carla has heard about a service that publishes books available in a variety of fonts thought to be amenable to dyslexic readers, and she has requested that the library purchase several volumes in this format.

## Step 1: Approachability

First, you want to make sure that Carla and Mohammed are comfortable contacting someone in the library with their requests. Iowa prescribes three strategies: smiling, establishing eye contact, and giving a greeting. However, as chapter 2 on communication discusses, these strategies may actually be off-putting to individuals with some types of disabilities. If the individual does not respond to these strategies, try alternatives, such as averting your gaze or waiting for them to continue the conversation. In addition, check with your accessibility resource people for suggestions of alternative means of welcoming individuals so that they can initiate accommodation requests using methods other than face-to-face contact. In particular, if you already provide or are considering alternative reference channels, such as phone, e-mail, or text message, make sure that these can be used for receiving accommodation requests as well. Also make sure that any of these alternative communication methods are publicized at the reference desk, on your website, and through other library publicity channels.

It is possible that some of your patrons may be so used to not finding accommodations that they may not even think to approach librarians with requests. Consider putting up signage and website information with messages such as "Ask us about our assistive technology, large print books, and other ease-of-access modifications" so that users know that accommodations already exist, possibly encouraging them to request others. Include information about all the ways that you can be contacted.

## Step 2: Interest

Iowa recommends offering a "confidential place to ask a question." This can be critical to any patron reluctant to reveal anything about the nature of his or her disability in a public area. It may also facilitate communication by providing a quiet environment outside the standard library hubbub—which turns out to be particularly important to Mohammed, who is slightly hard of hearing. The alternatives to face-to-face contact mentioned may also improve the patron's comfort around his or her communication being kept confidential.

## Step 3: Listening

Allow Mohammed to complete his initial statement without interrupting, even though you may be able to predict what he is trying to say. Not only is this courteous, but it also ensures that you will get a full picture of what he is seeking.

Carla tends to be verbose, and you notice that she is repeating her request multiple times. Try Iowa's suggestion of paraphrasing: "in your own words . . . without adding any thoughts or questions of your own." When she pauses, say something like "So you would like the library to purchase some books on gardening from X publisher that use a dyslexia-friendly font?"

## Step 4: Interviewing

People may request something that they have heard about without a full appreciation of its appropriateness either for their needs or for the library's ability to comply. In our second example, it is not yet clear what Carla's goal is and whether the books that she has requested will meet it.

Determining what will achieve the desired result is as relevant to accommodations as it is to information seeking. Iowa suggests asking open-ended questions, which "let the patrons tell you" more about what they want. For example, you might ask Carla which font that the publisher provides is most legible for her; among other things, this will let you know if she has been able to actually look at samples of what the publisher can provide. If she has not seen any samples, offer to show her the company's website. Avoid asking questions about the nature of her disability, which is unlikely to provide helpful information.

It may be useful to create a flowchart for staff to use in communicating with patrons about what accommodations are already available. A sample flowchart is provided in Figure 1.1; it is intended to help with interviews triggered by statements such as "The text on the computer is hard to read."

It is possible during this interview that the patron's question may change radically. For example, after looking at the publisher's website, Carla might decide that none of the fonts work for her, and what she really needs is to find a local professional who specializes in learning disabilities to help her find out what accommodations would be most effective for her.

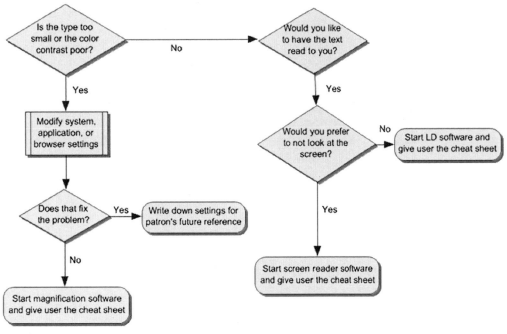

**Figure 1.1.** Sample flowchart for responding to patron inquiries.

## Step 5: Searching

In many situations, you will likely need some time to see if the accommodation is already provided by the library, if it is feasible, or if it may constitute a fundamental alteration. For Mohammed, you will need to see if a staff member has some time available to work with him and whether there are some mutually convenient times for them to meet. When you check your staff manual of community resources (see p. 10), you find that you do not have any learning disability professionals included, so you will need to do some research not only to help Carla but also to update the manual.

Keep both patrons posted regularly on your progress, via phone, e-mail, or another communication channel that is mutually agreeable to them and yourself. Be open to revisiting the interviewing step; for example, Mohammed may ask a question after the initial interview that requires additional discussion.

## Step 6: Answering

Providing a complete answer may or may not be the last step in the reference interview. In Mohammed's case, setting up a one-hour meeting with a staff member appears to fully address his request and is well within the bounds of what the library can provide. However, you may still want to do some follow-up with him after the meeting to ensure that his needs have been met.

## Step 7: Follow-Up

In addition to checking with the patrons to ensure they are satisfied, follow-up may involve showing them where something is located—especially in the case of assistive technology, providing assistance with getting the equipment started. For example, after Carla meets with the learning disability specialist, she contacts you again to let you know that he thought text-to-speech software (see chapter 6) meets her needs well and that she wants to use it at the library. If you already have such software on one or more computers, you can provide her with appropriate information and assistance to get started using it.

As part of your policy development (see next section), it may be necessary to determine if limitations need to be set on the amount of follow-up that the library is able to provide. This limitation should be equitable and clear and, wherever possible, provide alternative resources. This should make it easy to let Carla know that the library can provide up to two hours of initial support on software use and that a local assistive technology organization can provide more detailed classes and assistance at no charge to her.

Consider keeping track of user requests for accommodations that are not already available—especially those requiring significant funding or modifications—but that may still be considered reasonable. This information can be added to the information actively solicited from consulting resources to determine funding priorities and further assist with setting policies. If you do not yet have the software that Carla needs, ask her if the specialist recommended a particular product—this single input should inform but not necessarily dictate what you eventually acquire—and ask if she would be willing to be an accessibility resource person who can look at different options and help you make a decision about what software to buy.

## Creating Accessibility Policies

As you create an accessible environment, consistency and equity should be part of your goal. You do not want patrons feeling as though you accommodate quadriplegic people but not Deaf people nor perceiving some staff members to be helpful but others to be apathetic. Developing and enforcing policies can be useful ways to meet this goal.

Policies can help you cover a range of issues. For example, you may decide that you need policies to cover fair use of computers that are running adaptive technology. Given your library use patterns, do you need to have a policy that restricts use of these computers, or do you simply post signs asking that people who do not require assistive technology yield these computers on request?

Although you may find it useful to create a general policy on services to patrons with disabilities, also look at ways that existing policies can be modified. For example, accessibility resource people may volunteer that they or people they work with have difficulty finishing reading library books within the usual circulation period. The library might respond by creating a policy that, for materials not on a wait list, people with disabilities may be eligible for a longer borrowing period or may renew materials more times than normally allowed.

Some libraries have developed policies that require individuals to show proof of disability before they can take advantage of certain accommodations. This has always been legally murky—for example, the 2013 ADA settlement agreement with the Sacramento (CA) Public Library Authority, covering provision of accessible e-book readers (see chapter 6), specifically states, "The Library may not require proof of disability, including, for example, a doctor's note, before loaning the accessible e-reader devices to eligible patrons. However, the Library may require individuals who borrow the accessible e-reader devices to attest in writing that the accessible e-reader device is being borrowed by or for an eligible patron" ("Settlement Agreement" 2012). Talk to the library's legal counsel before including any proof-of-disability statements in your policies.

The *SPEC Kit 321: Services for Users with Disabilities* (Association of Research Libraries 2010) has many examples of forms, documentation, and policies that academic libraries have developed to serve patrons with disabilities. It also includes the results of a 2010 library poll on topics such as funding, responsibility for service provision and oversight, and publicizing services. Chapter 1 of *Implementing Cost-Effective Assistive Computer Technology* (Vincent 2012) has a template for developing policies around assistive technology that may be modified for use with other accessibility policies.

# ⑥ Staff Training

> The most valuable piece of equipment in a library to assist consumers with disabilities . . . is not equipment at all. It is a friendly, knowledgeable librarian. (Coombs 2000, 285)

Positive attitudes and accessibility awareness among library staff can be the most important way that your library can accommodate patrons with disabilities. The most likely way to empower your staff is by providing consistent and reinforced training about the library's approach toward accommodations. At a minimum, the training should cover etiquette and communication strategies (see chapter 2) as well as the policies, procedures, and resources specific to your library. Ideally, the training will also provide staff members with opportunities to provide input related to situations they have experienced or questions they have; these may be useful in further refining your library's accessibility strategy.

One tack that some training initiatives use is disability simulations—blindfolding trainees or having them try out a wheelchair to "see what it's like." Wright and Davie (1991, 7) point out the limitations of this: "Simulations *do not* give the true experience of most disabilities because when the game is over the individual can cease to be disabled. Persons with disabilities *live* with their disabling condition and learn to function in spite of that condition. They cannot suddenly stop being disabled." It may be a better strategy to involve disabled people in your training—perhaps start by inviting people with disabilities from your accessibility resource list—and ask them to provide experienced input about what does and does not work for them.

You may decide to provide training in-house, hire outside trainers, or do a combination of these. Chapter 8 of Courtney Deines-Jones and Connie Van Fleet's *Preparing Staff to Serve Patrons with Disabilities* (1995) provides a good overview of the pros and cons of various training options. It also highlights the importance of providing training for new staff and paraprofessionals.

If you have ongoing communication with staff—for example, a monthly newsletter or periodic e-mail—consider regularly including information about accessibility. This might be a tip about a creative way that a staff member has found to provide a particular accommodation—such as using large-print labels to make computer keyboards easier for elder patrons to see—an overview of new legislation likely to affect the library, a citation of a useful online resource, or a recently acquired book relating to disability culture.

Since it will be difficult for staff members to remember all relevant information related to accessibility even if it is reinforced on a regular basis through training, application, or both, it may be helpful to gather information into a staff manual that will be easy to consult on an as-needed basis. This manual might include:

- names and contact information for staff and consultants (e.g., the library's legal resource) with responsibility or expertise related to accessibility,
- cheat sheets for assistive technologies,
- procedural flowcharts (see p. 7), and
- description and contact information for outside resources.

At a minimum, this should include organizations that your accessibility resource people are involved with, as well as

- the nearest center for independent living—which can provide assistance with housing, employment, and so forth (for a directory, see http://www.ilru.org/html/publications/directory/index.html);
- the nearest senior center—check the phone book or do an online search; and
- the Tech ACT project, if one is available for your state/territory—which can provide information about funding for various types of assistive technology (for a directory, see http://assistivetech.net/webresources/stateTechActProjects.php).

Assume that this manual will need to be updated regularly. You may want to provide it primarily in an accessible electronic format, which will make it easier to share with the public if you choose to do so.

## Key Points

Your library's accessibility strategy should be built on a four-point foundation:

1. Active solicitation of input
2. Appropriate response to requests
3. Establishment of policies and procedures
4. Communication about all of these with all library staff

The majority of this book builds on that foundation by providing information related to areas most likely to generate accessibility considerations: communication, materials, architecture/environment, trainings/events, technology, and websites. We start in chapter 2 by looking at the keystone consideration: communication.

## References

ADA.gov. 2005. "Reaching Out to Customers with Disabilities. Lesson One: Policies, Practices, and Procedures." http://www.ada.gov/reachingout/lesson12.htm.
Association of Research Libraries. 2010. *SPEC Kit 321: Services for Users with Disabilities.* Washington, DC: Association of Research Libraries.
Coombs, Norman. 2000. "More than Technology." *Library Hi Tech News* 18, no. 3: 285–88.
Deines-Jones, Courtney, and Connie Van Fleet. 1995. *Preparing Staff to Serve Patrons with Disabilities.* New York: Neal-Schuman.

Department of Justice. 1993a. "The Americans with Disabilities Act Title II Technical Assistance Manual." http://www.ada.gov/taman2.html.

———. 1993b. "The Americans with Disabilities Act Title III Technical Assistance Manual." http://www.ada.gov/taman3.html.

Iowa Library Services, State Library of Iowa. 2013. "The Steps of the Reference Interview." http://www.statelibraryofiowa.org/ld/i-j/infolit/toolkit/geninfo/refinterview.

Murphy, Tish. 2007. *Library Furnishings: A Planning Guide.* Jefferson, NC: McFarland.

"Settlement Agreement between the United States of America, the National Federation of the Blind, and the Sacramento (California) Public Library Authority under the Americans with Disabilities Act." 2012. http://www.ada.gov/sacramento_ca_settle.htm.

Vincent, Jane. 2012. *Implementing Cost-Effective Assistive Computer Technology.* New York: Neal Schuman.

Wright, Kieth C., and Judith F. Davie. 1991. *Serving the Disabled.* New York: Neal Schuman.

## Resources

Flagg, R. 2013. "Focus Group Fundamentals for Government Programs." July 31. http://www.howto.gov/customer-experience/collecting-feedback/focus-group-fact-sheet.

Kulkarni, Manoj, and Neela J. Deshpande. 2012. "Empowering Library Users, Establishing Channel of Communication for Service Quality Expectations of Trainers from Government Administrative Training Institute (ATI) Libraries in India." Paper presented at the World Library and Information Congress: 78th IFLA General Conference and Assembly, Helsinki, Finland. http://conference.ifla.org/past/2012/203-kulkarni-en.pdf.

McNamara, Carter. 2013. "Basics of Conducting Focus Groups." http://managementhelp.org/businessresearch/focus-groups.htm.

SurveyMonkey. http://surveymonkey.com.

# CHAPTER 2

# Communication Accessibility

**— IN THIS CHAPTER —**

▷ Understanding conventions of disability etiquette

▷ Communicating with people who have different types of disabilities

▷ Being aware of auxiliary aids and services for communication

[My deafness] will affect how you communicate with me, yes it will and to deny that would be foolish, but the silence and sounds of my world do not define me as a person. They simply define the way in which we interact and they are but a lens that I place over my (already thick) glasses and see things. Because of these glasses however, I do see things that are more difficult for others. I am highly visual. I do very well in cultures that rely on nonverbal cues. (Nichols 2013)

EFFECTIVE COMMUNICATION BETWEEN PATRONS AND LIBRARY STAFF is a critical part of meeting library standards for quality service. As Felicia Yusuf (2011, 4) has noted, communication "is the bedrock of successful reference service and an avenue for understanding users' queries and meeting their information needs." The better the communication on both sides, the more likely it is that patrons will have positive experiences that will keep them coming back to your library.

As with all patrons, communicating with people with disabilities is facilitated by understanding and utilization of etiquette. This can help make patrons feel welcome as well as put library staff more at ease. For some people with disabilities, this will also require an understanding of alternative communication methods, including those that users bring with them and those provided by the library.

This chapter covers not only general etiquette tips but also information about communication strategies that people are likely to use or request. It intends to supplement information provided by members of your accessibility resource people (see chapter 1) and other current and potential library patrons.

## ◎ Basic Concepts for Communication

Even more than twenty years after the implementation of the ADA, it is possible that you and your staff members may not have had extensive experience interacting with people who have disabilities and so may feel discomfort at even the thought of such interactions. Shawn Lawton Henry (2007), a leading expert on web accessibility, has elegantly summed up two key reasons for this:

> One reason is that some people feel sorry for people with disabilities, and assume that they are bitter about their disabilities. This is untrue in many cases. Lots of people with disabilities feel that their lives are enriched by their experiences with disability, and even if given the chance to erase their disability would choose not to. . . . Another reason that some people are uncomfortable around people with disabilities is that they're afraid that they will "say the wrong thing." However, that's not a big deal to most people with disabilities. What's important is that you respect the person and see them beyond their disability.

Any individual's experience of disability is as idiosyncratic as his or her ethnicity, national origin, sexuality, or other traits. This covers both ability and attitude, making it impossible to accurately formulate sentences that begin "All blind people want to . . ." or "No Autistic people are able to . . ." Human ability runs on a continuum; for example, most people who consider themselves blind or Deaf have some amount of visual or auditory perception, even if it is not usable, and some quadriplegics have enough dexterity to use an alternative mouse, such as a trackball. In terms of attitude, people may run the gamut—from feeling as though their disability is something to be hidden at all costs to seeing it as something that shapes a cultural identity in which to take pride. The best strategy, therefore, is to remember the primary role of librarians in working with all patrons: "to facilitate the interactions between the potential information user community and the body of recorded information" (Kaliammal and Thamarai Selvi 2004, 184). Ask questions rather than make assumptions, and give individuals as much opportunity as possible to communicate their information seeking or other needs in their own way.

### Appropriate Language

As with other communities, there is ongoing debate about what is and what is not acceptable language for talking about disability. For example, a standard for many years has been "people-first" language—that is, mentioning the person and then the disability, such as "man with cerebral palsy" or "student with a brain injury." This is falling out of favor in some circles, however. Part of the reason may be the insistence of the media in mentioning disability when it is irrelevant in context—when was the last time that you read any mainstream articles about Stephen Hawking, who has ALS (amyotrophic lateral sclerosis), that did not make some reference to his body, wheelchair, or speech device?

The reaction may also come from individuals thinking about the implications of people-first language. C. Edwin Vaughan (2009) argued against people-first language for blind individuals: "To say, 'I am blind' or 'I am a blind person' no longer seems negative to many, particularly those groups with existential interest in the topic." Autism advocate

Ian Ford (2013) is one of many Autistic people who reject the construct: "Politically motivated terminology like person-first language builds shame around saying what one actually means, making it not only impossible to speak, but to even collect ones thoughts."

At this time, it is therefore difficult to make broad suggestions about what language is correct. (Note that this book uses various options throughout.) It is best to check with your accessibility resource people for guidance about regional and other factors in determining what language to recommend for use in library materials and interactions. You may also want to research and observe how people speak and write about themselves. For example, one trend is to capitalize the name of the disability type: "Deafness" has long been used to indicate identification with a Deaf culture, as opposed to the physical condition of "deafness," and "Autistic" is coming into wider usage among writers who distinguish themselves from "neurotypical" people who are not Autistic. Keep in mind, though, that overfocusing on specific language is ultimately unlikely to be as productive as cultivating a universally welcoming attitude, based on respect for the individual rather than on a stereotype.

There does need to be a strong distinction made between the acceptability of certain words when used among individuals with a shared disability and when used by outsiders. Listening to wheelchair users call each other "crip" or blind patrons refer to themselves as "blinks" does not mean that it is automatically alright for ambulatory or sighted people to use the same terms.

## Communication Etiquette

Much of the etiquette of communicating with people who have disabilities overlaps with general politeness: do offer people options rather than assuming what they will want; do let people finish their sentences; do not condescend. The most basic rule, however, can also be the hardest to master: relax. It is usually fine to use common phrases such as "see you later" when speaking to a blind person. It is never fine to let being so nervous about saying something incorrect that you miss the opportunity for effective communication.

Beyond that, there are some basic etiquette considerations specific to interactions with patrons who have or might have a disability:

- If the patron is accompanied by a companion, such as an attendant or interpreter, make sure that you are still looking at and talking directly to the patron when you are communicating with him or her, even if the companion is speaking for the patron. (Of course, keep in mind that the companion also deserves your patience and politeness.)
- If someone seems uncomfortable with what you believe to be a standard communication component (e.g., making eye contact), try to adapt what you are doing. Go with your gut. In some cases, you will sense that it is alright to ask the person what she or he would like you to do differently; in other cases, you may need to use some trial and error.
- Assistive technology should be treated with the same respect as the person. For example, just as you would not lean on someone's shoulder while you are talking to them, do not lean on someone's wheelchair.
- Consider the situation in context. Stephen Hawking is said to have loved having his speech device aped by actors on *The Big Bang Theory*, but he might not feel the same about imitations from random bystanders.

A combination of the golden rule and common sense will go a long way in facilitating your interactions. Unwarranted personal questions and unsolicited advice are as inappropriate in communicating with disabled people as they are in any other library situation. Disability advocate David Roche (2008, 110), who has a facial disfigurement, describes a particularly uncomfortable encounter that serves as a model of poor communication:

> One of the librarians [in a hospital library] came up to me as I was bent over my books. She said, "I thought you might be interested in this," and set in front of me a booklet entitled *The Let's Face It Resource Guide for People with Facial Difference*. She quickly walked away. I was angry and embarrassed. I brought the booklet home and showed it to [my wife] Marlena. I told her, "I want nothing to do with this."

## ⑥ Auxiliary Aids and Services

Title II and Title III of the ADA discuss the responsibility to provide auxiliary aids and services intended to facilitate communication. Several examples are provided in both titles, including materials in alternative formats (see chapter 3), assistive listening devices, interpreters, note takers, braille, and magnification software (Department of Justice 2010). In an accurate prediction, the guidance also states, "It is not possible to provide an exhaustive list (of examples), and an attempt to do so would omit the new devices that will become available with emerging technology."

Libraries usually find it more effective to be responsive to accommodation requests rather than anticipate what any patron might need. The ADA is clear that while a Title II or Title III entity should try to provide the specific accommodation requested, it has the right to choose among different, equally effective aids and services if the requested type would cause either a fundamental alteration or an undue burden. The authors of the 2010 ADA revision are also clear that covered entities do not need to anticipate or provide every possible type of accommodation.

The best overall strategy is still the one stated by Kovalik and Kruppenbacher (1994, 1): "Individuals requesting auxiliary aids or services, and places of public accommodation are encouraged to work together so that individuals receive an adequate level of service and places of public accommodation comply with the law." The Indiana State Library (2013) has published a model policy statement about its provision of auxiliary aids and services that covers legal implications, procedures for requesting and receiving accommodations, and record keeping.

The Department of Justice recognized in the preamble to the 1991 Title II regulation that the list of auxiliary aids was "not an all-inclusive or exhaustive catalogue of possible or available auxiliary aids or services. It is not possible to provide an exhaustive list, and an attempt to do so would omit the new devices that will become available with emerging technology" (28 CFR part 35, app. A at 560, 2009). This view has not been changed. However, neither should the inclusion of a list of examples in the definition of "auxiliary aids" be read as a requirement for a Title II entity to offer every possible auxiliary aid listed in the definition in every situation (Department of Justice 2010).

## Simple Communication Strategies

In a world of high tech, it is often easy to forget that there are low- and no-tech tools that can facilitate communication. In many cases, simple communication methods, such as pointing or writing, still work fine, as either a temporary or an ongoing strategy for a given patron. Creating a couple of communication boards will be helpful for many situations, including interacting with people for whom English is a second language as well as people with disabilities that affect communication. Confer with library staff about the most common questions that people ask and with your accessibility resource people about additional topics that they think might be important to include. For areas of the library, consider using photos of the location or placing the same icon that is used on the board somewhere prominent within the area—for example, on the front of the reference desk or the door of the children's room. Figure 2.1 is a sample board; the images are from the clip art library included with Microsoft Word and from the Oakland Public Library's "Dewey Pictograms" (California Library Literacy Services 2013).

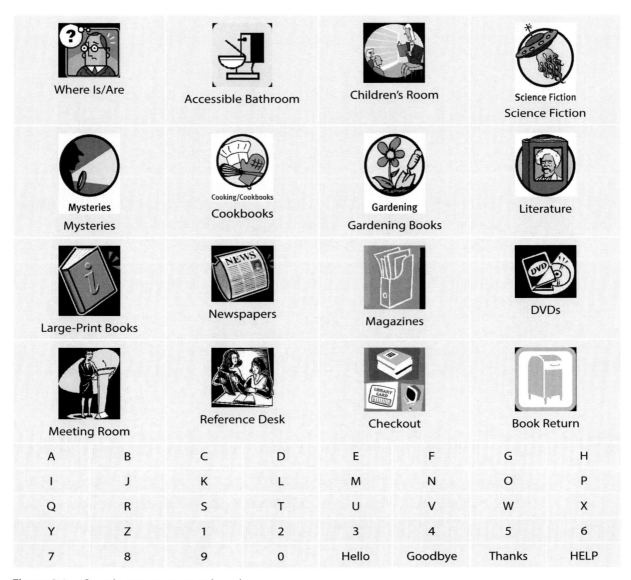

**Figure 2.1.** Sample communication board.

# ⊚ Communication Strategies with Different Patron Contingents

While etiquette goes a long way in facilitating communication, knowing something about different types of communication strategies is helpful. The following information provides an overview to assist in face-to-face interactions with patrons who might have a variety of disabilities.

## Communicating with Patrons Who Are Deaf or Hard of Hearing

In popular American concepts of Deafness, everyone uses American Sign Language. This is a fallacy. Many people use no type of manual communication, and some may use different manual languages, such as Signed Exact English, which is a word-for-word translation of English rather than a separate language.

American Sign Language is as nuanced and complex as any other language, including slang, regional variations, and puns. It also has some unique features, such as a spatially based way for communicating directions that is much more efficient and elegant than "Well, first you turn left, and then, uh . . ." Work with any speakers of manual languages among your accessibility resource people to come up with a basic vocabulary that library staff should know and recognize—some universals might be "Where is the bathroom?" and "Where is the checkout?"

It is also a fallacy to assume that lip-reading provides sufficient accuracy for detailed communication. For English, this has much to do with letter pairs that sound different but look the same when pronounced—as in /b/ and /p/, such that words like "batter" and "patter" will be indistinguishable. Moustaches, poor lighting, and even regionality can provide further complications. The late Chicago journalist Henry Kisor (1990, xiii) wrote, "I have found that New Yorkers, who speak as fast as they can while moving their lips as little as possible, are exceptionally difficult to understand, while American Southerners of both sexes seem warmly expressive, relaxed, and easy to lipread." Ask your accessibility resource people what fallback options are preferable when lip-reading fails.

The biggest innovation in communication in the last ten years for people who do not hear is also the most mainstream: text messaging. Texting has a myriad of benefits over older telephone alternatives. It is immediate, and people with and without hearing can use the same hardware. It is also transparent. As a contributor to the DeafTimes blog noted, "for the deaf, communication with the hearing world, especially those who do not sign, has been difficult. Now, with the advent of texting, deaf people can communicate with the larger world in exactly the same way as their peers" (Ray 2010). If you provide services such as reference or homework assistance via texting, talk with Deaf and hard-of-hearing people in your accessibility resource group to figure out the best way to let people know that this is available. Keep in mind that texting may also be an option for real-time face-to-face interactions.

For people who cannot or do not text, free speech-to-speech service is available nationwide. A person who uses an older, specialized communication system, such as a text telephone, can call 711 to reach a trained operator, who then contacts the requested person or organization and acts as an interpreter. This service also allows hearing people to initiate the call; a list of toll-free numbers is available at http://www.speechtospeech.org/support.html. Make sure that any staff members responsible for fielding phone calls are aware that someone may use speech-to-speech to call them.

For people who speak manual languages, video relay services (VRS) can be used to communicate with speech-to-speech operators, also known as communication assistants.

Instead of typing, VRS users communicate via an Internet-based video link. As the Federal Communications Commission (2013) notes, "because the conversation between the VRS user and the communication assistants flows much more quickly than with a text-based [telecommunications relay service] call, VRS has become an enormously popular form of [telecommunication]." A list that includes VRS providers is at http://www.fcc.gov/encyclopedia/trs-providers.

For public events and meetings (see chapter 5), there are multiple types of accommodation strategies. First, people who speak American Sign Language may request sign language interpreters. For any event that runs much longer than twenty minutes, it is customary to hire two interpreters so that they can trade off (unlike conversational signing, nonstop interpreting does not organically incorporate pauses and can therefore be hard on the wrists). A searchable registry of American Sign Language interpreters who are members of the Registry of Interpreters for the Deaf is available at https://www.rid.org/acct-app/index.cfm?action=search.members. Deaf members of your group of accessibility resource people may also be able to suggest local agencies or freelance interpreters.

Second, computer-assisted real-time translation (CART) is similar to courtroom stenography, except that the text being typed is displayed on either a large screen or a private computer monitor. Like stenography, it also requires a trained typist who can transcribe spoken language with appropriate speed and accuracy. A list of questions to ask a potential CART provider is at http://cart-info.org/questions.html; if appropriate, you may also want to ask if the provider is willing to furnish a post facto transcript of the event for distribution via website or other means. A list of certified CART providers is at http://www.stenosearch.com/_connect/cart_reporters.htm.

Third, voice interpreters use exaggerated mouth movements, body language, and gestures to convey spoken language to some people who do not use sign language. People who have been trained to provide voice interpretation may hold an oral transliteration certificate from the Registry of Interpreters for the Deaf. To find certificate holders, go to the searchable registry just listed and choose "OTC" (for Oral Transliteration Certificate) from the "Certificates" pull-down list.

Finally, cued speech is a type of voice interpretation that uses specific hand shapes and hand placement to help lip-readers distinguish between similar letters, such as /p/ and /b/. Check with local Deafness organizations to find cued speech interpreters.

A frequently asked question is whether speech input software (see chapter 6) can be used to provide transcripts. While this might someday be possible, the technology is not yet sophisticated enough to recognize random voices speaking quickly, emotionally, or in other ways that thwart accurate recognition. It is also not able to identify who said what, which is a feature that is easy to provide with CART.

The 2010 revision of the ADA explicitly includes video remote interpreting (VRI) as a type of auxiliary aid and service. When two people in the same location need American Sign Language or other types of interpreting services and an interpreter cannot be physically present, VRI can be used to gain access to an interpreter at a call center via the Internet. The Federal Communications Commission (2013) explicitly states that VRI and VRS are different and that VRS cannot be used to provide VRI. A list of VRI providers is available at http://clearviewinnovations.com/vri_info.html.

## Communicating with Blind Patrons

People who see are really, really focused on seeing. We use a lot of visual markers in our communications: pointing, facial expressions, body language. The hardest thing for us to do is to communicate visual concepts in nonvisual terms. If you are doing this informally, it can be an interesting challenge. If, however, you are trying to give directions or communicate other information to a patron, it can be frustrating to both sides.

The Chicago Lighthouse has a splendid guide entitled "How to Communicate with Someone Who Is Blind" (2013), which opens with, "Don't feel overly conscious or obsess about being politically correct when talking to someone who is blind." It also includes several practical tips—for instance, "Identify yourself when someone who is blind or visually impaired enters a room or when you are approaching the person" and "Direct questions or comments directly to the person who is blind or visually impaired, not to someone they are with." Note that this guide does recommend use of people-first language, thereby demonstrating that there is no consensus on what is appropriate.

## Communicating with Patrons with Speech Disabilities

As with any other patron, it is good etiquette to allow someone who speaks slowly or with difficulty to finish without interruption. However, it is also considered polite to let someone know when you do not understand him or her; asking someone to repeat what he or she said is generally considered less offensive than simply smiling and nodding.

The speech-to-speech service mentioned earlier also has operators who are skilled in interpreting nonstandard speech. There have been some experiments using VRS to facilitate this; if the operator can see the person speaking, it may be easier for her or him to know what is being said.

Some people with speech disabilities use augmentative/alternative communication devices. These might take the form of simple communication boards, sophisticated electronic tools, or something in between. Augmentative/alternative communication devices usually provide words, pictures, audio output, or some combination of these that the user can invoke to serve as his or her voice. Respond to such communication as if it were vocal, including requests that users repeat what they said if necessary. Be aware that augmentative/alternative communication users may also use synthesized speech devices to communicate via telephone, without using speech-to-speech as a go-between; make an effort to understand the device, but be honest if you cannot hear what is being said.

## Communicating with Autistic Patrons

If you meet one person with autism, you've met one person with autism. (Dr. Stephen Shore, a special education teacher who is himself Autistic; Elwood 2009, 1)

It is not clear whether the incidence of autism has increased exponentially or it is just the public's awareness of it. In either case, Autistic people are continuing to gain visibility within society, including that as library patrons. As with other types of disabilities, a particular person's level of autism may or may not require accommodations.

The Scotch Plains Public Library and Fanwood Memorial Library (both in New Jersey) have put together a resource for librarians about communicating with Autistic patrons (see http://www.librariesandautism.org/index.htm). The center of this resource is a nineteen-minute training video designed to put librarians at ease. Tips from this video include the following:

- "Speak directly, simply, and slowly" but "don't be condescending."
- "Try to make eye contact," but be aware that patrons may not respond.
- "Avoid open-ended questions"—questions that can be answered yes/no may be more effective.
- "Give a tour" to new patrons.
- Ignore repetitive behaviors: "rocking, humming, pacing, or wiggling."
- Don't ignore "destructive activities, violent tantrums, loud or inappropriate interactions with others, and inappropriate sexual behavior." Instead, "offer to help the caregiver, sit next to the person with autism, offer to relocate other patrons," and, if necessary, follow standard emergency procedures.
- "Be an ambassador" to people with autism, modeling appropriate interactions to other patrons.

The presenters point out that much of this information is simply best practice. "As you listen to these tips, you may realize how universal these strategies can be in dealing with any library patron."

The Libraries and Autism website also includes templates for *This Is My Library*, a book that can be customized for people with autism to review before coming to the library and for a communication board that has been designed to facilitate interactions in other situations, as with nonnative speakers of English.

Interaction badges or stickers are coming into use by Autistic people to indicate how communicative they are feeling: no badge, "I'm open to initiating or responding to conversation"; green badge, "I need you to start a conversation"; yellow badge, "Only talk to me if I already know you"; red badge, "Please don't initiate a conversation" (Sibley 2012). Check with your Autistic accessibility resource people and see if they would like you to provide interaction badges for people to use on an ad hoc basis. Colored stickers are available in the label section of any office supply store and can be provided for this purpose. Consider cutting the stickers into different shapes or providing other redundant visual cues so that the meaning is also communicated to color-blind people.

Communication at a deeper level may also be useful, since the unspoken rules of library behavior may not be obvious to Autistic people—or children, or people unused to visiting the library, or many other groups. Ian Ford (2013), in an essay covering many aspects of accommodation, provides a suggestion specific to libraries:

> There is a scheme for using a library, that most people know only because they have been taught it explicitly: you browse for as long as you want; you are allowed to read books in the library without checking them out; you are not supposed to re-shelve them yourself; and so on. An accessible library might prominently explain that scheme and not just expect people to know.

Check with your accessibility resource people to see what might be useful to include as part of an explanation relevant to your library and how they would like this explanation to be distributed.

## Communicating with People Demonstrating Unusual Behavior

There are a variety of reasons why someone might be acting unusually within the library, including drug/alcohol use or excessive stress. Rhea Joyce Rubin (2011, 76), in her invaluable book *Defusing the Angry Patron*, provides a strategy for interactions in these situations:

> If patrons display behaviors typical of substance abuse or mental illness but do not seem ill and are not bothering anyone, there is no need to approach them. But if their behaviors are disturbing other patrons, or if they appear to be sick, you must talk to them. If possible, bring a coworker with you. Ask "Are you okay?" or "Do you need medical assistance?" Call for an ambulance if a patron needs help. If the person does not want medical assistance or does not seem ill, focus on the disruptive behavior as you would with any other patron.

The San Francisco Public Library is one of a few places that have enhanced its community service by having a social worker and five peer counselors on staff. These staff members approach individuals who may need social services. Several years into the program, this seems to be working well: patrons feel respected, and librarians are freed to perform their standard tasks (Nieves 2013).

However, this does not address the needs of someone with Tourette's syndrome who wants to attend a library event despite his or her loud auditory tics or someone with obsessive-compulsive disorder whose involuntary rituals might include something like repeatedly counting books aloud in an area where others are trying to study. The best strategy is likely to work with the individual to see what accommodations might have worked for him or her in other situations and what creative strategies will be appropriate for both the individual and the library.

## Key Points

The etiquette may be a bit different and the communication methods initially unfamiliar, but patrons with disabilities ultimately have the same library communications needs as nondisabled patrons: they may want information on finding a job; they may hope to get on the waiting list for an interesting biography; or they are just looking for a convenient bathroom. Once "how to" communication issues are addressed, focus on the patron's need for information rather than on his or her disability.

A likely topic about which any patron will want to communicate is materials provided by the library—books, DVDs, and so forth. We talk about factors affecting accessibility to these in chapter 3.

## References

Chicago Lighthouse for People Who Are Blind or Visually Impaired. 2013. "How to Communicate with Someone Who Is Blind." http://chicagolighthouse.org/programs-and-services/working-someone-who-blind-or-visually-impaired/how-communicate-someone-who-bli.

Department of Justice. 2010. "Americans with Disabilities Act Title II Regulations Part 35 Nondiscrimination on the Basis of Disability in State and Local Government Services (as Amended by the Final Rule Published on September 15, 2010)." http://www.ada.gov/ regs2010/titleII_2010/titleII_2010_regulations.htm.

Elwood, Heather. 2009. "Teaching Children with Autism Spectrum Disorders." *EDCompass Newsletter*, October, 1–4.

Federal Communications Commission. 2013. "Video Relay Services." http://www.fcc.gov/guides/ video-relay-services.

Ford, Ian. 2013. "Deep Accessibility." Ian Ford (blog). September 6. http://ianology.wordpress .com/2013/09/06/deep-accessibility/.

Henry, Shawn Lawton. 2007. "The Basics: Interacting with People with Disabilities." http://www .uiaccess.com/accessucd/interact.html.

Indiana State University. 2013. "Policy for Ensuring Effective Communications with Individuals with Disabilities." http://in.gov/library/files/Policy_for_Ensuring_Effective_Communica tions_with_Individiuals_with_Disabilities.pdf.

Kaliammal, A., and G. Thamarai Selvi. 2004. "The Virtual Library: Changing Roles and Ethical Challenges for Librarians." Paper presented at CALIBER 2004, New Delhi (India), February 11–13. http://eprints.rclis.org/15232/1/04cali_24.pdf.

Kisor, Henry. 1990. *What's That Pig Outdoors?* New York: Hill & Wang.

Kovalik, Gail, and Frank Kruppenbacher. 1994. "Libraries and the ADA: Providing Accessible Media to Deaf and Hard-of-Hearing People." *MC Journal: The Journal of Academic Media Librarianship* 2, no. 1: 1–19. http://wings.buffalo.edu/publications/mcjrnl/v2n1/kovalik.html.

Nichols, Meriah. 2013. "Down Syndrome: More Alike Than Different . . . and Yet." With a Little Moxie (blog). July 3. http://www.withalittlemoxie.com/blog/down-syndrome-more-alike-than-different-and-yet/.

Nieves, Evelyn. 2013. "Public Libraries: The New Homeless Shelters." Salon.com. March 7. http:// www.salon.com/2013/03/07/public_libraries_the_new_homeless_shelters_partner/.

Ray. 2010. "Texting: A New Way for Deaf to Communicate." DeafTimes (blog). August 3. http:// deaftimes.com/usa-l/texting-a-new-way-for-deaf-to-communicate/.

Roche, David. 2008. *The Church of 80% Sincerity*. New York: Perigee.

Rubin, Rhea Joyce. 2011. *Defusing the Angry Patron*. 2nd ed. New York: Neal-Schuman.

Sibley, Kassiane. 2012. "I Wish the Whole World Had Interaction Badges." Thinking Person's Guide to Autism (blog). July 11. http://www.thinkingautismguide.com/2012/07/i-wish-whole-world-had-interaction.html.

Vaughan, C. Edwin. 2009. "People-First Language: An Unholy Crusade." *Braille Monitor*. March. https://nfb.org/images/nfb/publications/bm/bm09/bm0903/bm090309.htm.

Yusuf, Felicia. 2011. "Effective Communication for Reference Service Delivery in Academic Libraries." *Library Philosophy and Practice*, June, 1–5.

## ⑥ Resources

### Communicating with People Who Are Deaf/ Hard of Hearing or Have Speech Disabilities

Computer-assisted real-time translation providers: http://www.stenosearch.com/_connect/cart_ reporters.htm. (A list of questions to ask a potential provider is at http://cart-info.org/ questions.html.)

Registry of Interpreters for the Deaf: https://www.rid.org/acct-app/index.cfm?action=search .members.

Speech-to-speech: http://www.speechtospeech.org/ (or dial 711).

Video relay services providers: http://www.fcc.gov/encyclopedia/trs-providers.

Video remote interpreter providers: http://clearviewinnovations.com/vri_info.html.

## Communicating with Autistic People

Brown, Lydia. 2011. "The Significance of Semantics: Person-First Language—Why It Matters." Autistic Hoya (blog). August 4. http://www.autistichoya.com/2011/08/significance-of-semantics-person-first.html.

Scotch Plains Public Library (NJ) and Fanwood Memorial Library (NJ). 2013. "Libraries and Autism: We're Connected." http://www.librariesandautism.org/index.htm.

## Miscellaneous

California Library Literacy Services. 2013. "Dewey Pictograms." http://libraryliteracy.org/staff/differences/dewey.html.

# Materials Accessibility

OVER THE PAST THIRTY OR SO YEARS, there has been a dizzying increase in the variety of formats in which a library might provide materials. When new formats become available, many libraries try to provide these formats to their patrons in as timely a manner as budgets and other practical considerations allow. This has resulted in complications such as the reluctance of some publishers to allow libraries to purchase and check out e-books, as well as the higher cost of Blu-ray discs when compared to DVDs.

Materials accessibility provides another complication. There are two basic reasons why materials may not be accessible: either the format itself has inherent barriers, or the creators of a given item have not followed published guidelines for making it accessible. Providing equitable access is also complicated by the challenges of copyright law, which continues to evolve.

While the National Library Service for the Blind and Physically Handicapped continues to serve many people by providing a limited number of materials in accessible formats, it does not substitute for the obligation of mainstream libraries to accommodate patrons with disabilities. A statement published by the Association of Specialized and Cooperative Library Agencies in 2001 says, "Equity of access to information is, or should be, at least as important as ramps, entry doors and bathrooms. The ADA is civil rights legislation."

This chapter provides an overview of the current state of materials accessibility, in terms both legal and technical. It also provides guidance on how to maximize the accessibility of these materials, whether generated by or simply provided by the library.

## ◎ What Is Print Disability?

Print disability was initially defined in terms of sight impairment. In 1931, the Pratt-Smoot Act was passed: "an act to provide books for the adult blind." This established what is now the National Library Service for the Blind and Physically Handicapped. The law has been amended multiple times since then, most notably in 1952 to include children and in 1966 to include individuals "certified by competent authority as unable to read normal printed material as a result of physical limitations," such as quadriplegics (FindLaw 2013).

In 1996, public law No. 104-197, commonly known as the Chafee amendment, was passed, stating that "it is not an infringement of copyright for an authorized entity to reproduce or to distribute copies or phonorecords of a previously published, nondramatic literary work if such copies or phonorecords are reproduced or distributed in specialized formats exclusively for use by blind or other persons with disabilities" (National Library Service for the Blind and Physically Handicapped 2010). The amendment references Pratt-Smoot to define print disability.

Unfortunately, these laws were written before there was a wide understanding of the role that alternative formats can play in accommodating people with learning and other types of cognitive disabilities. As noted in chapter 6, many people find it difficult to interpret information presented only in print or audio format, but they do well with information presented simultaneously in both formats. Their ability to access an audio version of materials generally provided only in print, or vice versa, can be a critical accommodation but is not yet as widely accepted as accommodations for the inability to see or hold printed materials, and cognitive disabilities are not necessarily mentioned in current legislation.

A good indicator of current thinking on what legally constitutes a print disability comes from Bookshare (http://www.bookshare.org), a service that provides materials in electronic format to individuals with disabilities. To ensure that they are within the bounds of fair use for copyrighted materials, Bookshare requires that subscribers provide proof of "physically-based disability," which includes learning or reading disabilities. It explicitly does not include intellectual disabilities, attention-deficit disorder, emotional disabilities, and so forth, "unless accompanied by a qualifying visual, physical, learning or reading disability" (Bookshare 2013).

Does this mean that libraries are policing who does and does not have a print disability? Not when services are offered to the public at large. For example, according to a survey published in 2005, most libraries that provide self-service scanning offer them to any user for any purpose (Caswell and Freund 2005). If users cannot perform the scanning themselves, public libraries might offer some general help—such as that indicated in the Skokie (IL) Public Library's (2013) statement "Patron Technology Assistants can provide basic assistance for scanning"—but they might also consider the scanning of large amounts of materials to be an undue burden. Academic libraries, however, may develop policies such as the one used by the University of California–Berkeley (2013), which scans circulating, reference, and interlibrary loan books for students but requires proof of disability.

Note that Bookshare's requirement of proof of disability also means that libraries cannot purchase Bookshare subscriptions for use by unspecified patrons, although patrons with their own subscriptions should be able to access materials from library computers. Bookshare also partners with OverDrive on the Library e-Book Accessibility Program to provide free one-year Bookshare memberships with limited access for patrons of libraries that subscribe to the e-book distributor OverDrive; however, these patrons still need to provide proof of disability. More information about the program is available at https://www.bookshare.org/_/promo/2010/01/overDrive.

# ⑥ Legislation

Copyright doesn't graft well onto—what's that term? Oh, yeah—reality. (Jack Bernard, associate general counsel, University of Michigan; quoted in irinazey 2012)

Copyright law in general can be confusing, and a comprehensive mandate that balances the rights of copyright holders and people with print disabilities has yet to be worked out. While the following information provides an overview of current thought, you will likely want to check with your legal counsel regarding any specific situations.

## Fair Use

Section 107 of U.S. copyright law defines four factors to be considered when determining whether "the use made of a work in any particular case is a fair use":

(1) the purpose and character of the use, including whether such use is of a commercial nature or is for nonprofit educational purposes;
(2) the nature of the copyrighted work;
(3) the amount and substantiality of the portion used in relation to the copyrighted work as a whole; and
(4) the effect of the use upon the potential market for or value of the copyrighted work. (U.S. Copyright Office 2013)

The University of Texas has created a Copyright Crash Course website (http://copyright.lib.utexas.edu) that further refines the definition of fair use, based on litigation, into two considerations: "Is the use you want to make of another's work transformative—that is, does it add value to and repurpose the work for a new audience—and is the amount of material you want to use appropriate to achieve your transformative purpose?" (University of Texas Libraries 2007).

In 2012, the Hathi Trust (http://www.hathitrust.org), a digital repository of materials scanned from research libraries, successfully defended its right in federal court to provide materials under fair use (Albanese 2012). According to Kenneth Crews (2012) from Columbia University, the Hathi ruling finally established that mainstream libraries and universities should indeed be considered "authorized entities" under the Chafee amendment.

Crews also says that the Hathi ruling established that fair use covers both fiction and non-fiction and that "maintaining copies of entire works [in transformed formats] was justified for the purposes of serving print-disabled persons."

It would be easy to assume that everyone sees fair use as a given, but that has not been the case; several entities maintain that it goes too far in altering patent rights. As of this writing, the Hathi Trust ruling is being appealed by the Authors Guild. In addition, the United States has yet to sign the World Intellectual Property Association's "International Instrument/Treaty on Limitations and Exceptions for Visually Impaired Persons/Persons with Print Disabilities." In April 2013, the Intellectual Property Owners Association, which represents "companies and individuals in all industries and fields of technology who own, or are interested in, intellectual property rights," sent a letter to the director of the U.S. Patent Office opposing the World Intellectual Property Association treaty on the grounds that it would be a "precedent for establishing broad exceptions and limitations to patent rights without adequate protections for innovators." Stay tuned . . .

## Noncopyrighted Materials

Materials that are no longer in copyright are considered to be in the public domain and are not subject to any restrictions related to creating alternative formats. There are multiple initiatives to convert books in the public domain to electronic or other alternative formats; the best known of these is probably Project Gutenberg (http://www.gutenberg.org), which provides access to a range of classic fiction and nonfiction, from *Alice in Wonderland* and *On the Origin of Species* to *The Gay Gnani of Gingalee* and *Fungi: Their Nature and Uses*. The Hathi Trust and Bookshare sites mentioned earlier include both copyrighted and noncopyrighted materials; anyone can access materials in the latter category. The University of Pennsylvania maintains a searchable database of all books available online for free. This database, which appears to be updated daily, is at http://onlinebooks.library.upenn.edu. Another good resource is the Unchained board on Pinterest at http://www.pinterest.com/rosefirerising/unchained-finding-free-books/.

## Overview of Formatting Accessibility

Materials accessibility, like web accessibility (see chapter 7), is primarily defined by two considerations: whether it is compatible with assistive technologies and whether it is innately accessible to people who have access needs but do not use assistive technologies. The more complex the format, the more problems it is likely to pose and the more difficult it may be to change into a different format. This section looks at the issues for print, electronic, and multimedia formats that libraries are most likely to produce or acquire for patron use.

## Large Print

Large print is a format that has long been common for libraries to carry. In 2002, Robert Dahlin wrote that "a huge market for large-print books seems inevitable," hypothesizing that aging boomers and computer eyestrain would sustain demand. An article published nine years later presented a murkier picture, less because of the proliferation of electronic formats than the effect of the recession on library budgets (Bond 2011). Check with your low-vision accessibility resource people (see chapter 1), including elders, to see if they find large print to be a preferred format or if e-books satisfy their reading needs.

## Standard Print

An alternative to large print is the provision of CCTVs (closed-circuit televisions), also known as video magnifiers. These are devices that focus on print materials placed on a movable bed and enlarge them on the fly to a display, which is either a built-in screen or the monitor of a nearby computer. The image is not saved as it would be if optical character recognition (OCR) were used (see p. 30), but it can handle formats that scanners cannot, such as handwriting. CCTVs may also be used to make it easier for people with low vision to perform fine handwork, such as needlepoint or fishing fly tying. Figure 3.1 is a photo of a typical desktop CCTV.

A desktop CCTV will cost around $3,000, but there are now many portable models available for under $1,000; some have optional stands if hands-free use is needed. A few desktop models now have additional capabilities, such as the ability to reformat text into

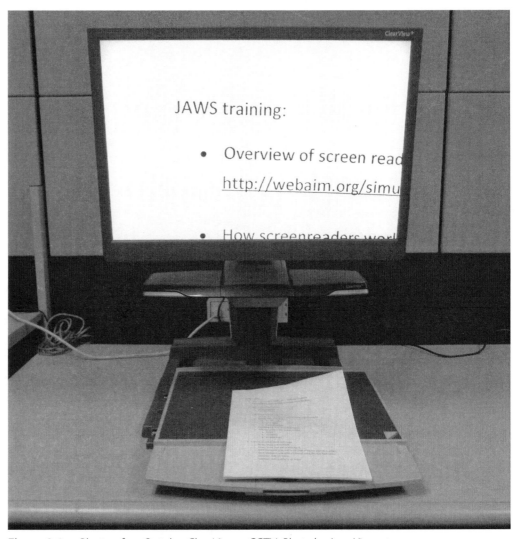

**Figure 3.1.** Photo of an Optelec ClearView+ CCTV. *Photo by Jane Vincent*

columns that eliminate the need to constantly readjust the bed. Your accessibility resource people may have experience with particular models that they would recommend or strong preferences about features they would like a library-provided CCTV to have. Used models may also be available through your local assistive technology reuse center (a list is available at http://www.passitoncenter.org) or through mainstream boards such as Craigslist.

For individuals who need to convert print materials into electronic text for compatibility with their assistive technology, scanners paired with OCR software such as OmniPage will do the trick. Specialized OCR programs for use by individuals with visual disabilities are available for Windows, including OpenBook (http://www.freedomscientific.com/products/fs/openbook-product-page.asp) and Kurzweil 1000 (http://www.kurzweiledu.com/kurzweil-1000-v13-windows.html). These tend to be quite expensive, and you will want to get feedback from your blind patrons about whether they have used these programs and find them valuable. Alternatively, you may want to get their recommendations for mainstream OCR programs that work well with screen readers.

Keep in mind that the quality and complexity of the original materials will affect the quality of the scanned materials. Items may not scan well if they have poor contrast between text and background colors or if they are a copy of a copy of a copy of an original. OCR programs may also have problems converting mathematical formulas, tables, dingbats, columns, and other elements.

You may want to provide a statement near each scanner and on your website informing people about fair use and asking them to respect it. North Carolina State University uses the following:

> The copyright law of the United States (Title 17, United States Code) governs the making of photocopies or other reproductions of copyrighted material. Under certain conditions specified in the law, libraries and archives are authorized to furnish a photocopy or other reproduction. One of these specified conditions is that the photocopy or other reproduction is not to be "used for any purpose other than private study, scholarship, or research." If a user makes a request for, or later uses, a photocopy or reproduction for purpose in excess of "fair use," that user may be liable for copyright infringement. (Caswell and Freund 2005, 83)

If you have a file that has been scanned as an image (e.g., by using the Fax and Scan program built into recent versions of Windows), there are free OCR conversion programs available on the Internet that can turn these files into editable text. Instead of saving the converted text into a file, these programs usually save the text into a box on their website that can then be copied and pasted into your word processor of choice. An online search for "free online OCR" should result in a list of currently available services; New OCR (http://www.newocr.com) is one that has been shown to work well.

If users want to convert electronic text into an audio format and save the resulting file as an MP3 or in another popular format, there are free resources online, including YAKiToMe! (http://www.yakitome.com/tts/text_to_speech), Text2Speech (http://www.text2speech.org), and vozMe (http://vozme.com/index.php?lang=en). Software programs designed to provide assistance for people with learning disabilities (see chapter 6) may also provide a text-to-audio conversion capability.

## Braille

Although it is often assumed that all blind people use braille, in reality the numbers are quite low. Search online for "percentage blind braille users" and the first page of results shows estimates ranging from 4% to 12% of blind children learning braille. People who became blind as adults are even less likely to use braille, either because they find other strategies satisfactory (e.g., audio output) or because common causes of blindness, including diabetes or HIV, may also affect tactile sensitivity. However, people who use braille find advantages, including portability and accuracy (it is much easier to know if a word is spelled correctly if you are reading it rather than hearing it), and studies tend to show a correlation between braille use and employability. Braille is also available in several forms, including Uncontracted or Grade 1 (letter-for-letter equivalent of print text), Contracted or Grade 2 (represents common words or letter combinations in a single character, increasing reading efficiency), and specialized code sets for math, music, science, and so on. Check with your accessibility resource people to see if there are braille users in your community and what their needs are.

If you decide to provide the ability for staff or patrons to do in-house braille printing, you will need to invest in at least two components: an embosser to print the braille and software to translate information from text into an electronic form that the embosser can recognize. Figure 3.2 shows a lower-end embosser that can sit on a tabletop and that costs around $2,500; there are also many higher-end embossers that

**Figure 3.2.** Romeo Attaché braille printer. *Photo by Jane Vincent*

are free-standing and considerably more expensive. In 2001, the National Federation of the Blind created a good guide to selecting a braille printer, available at https://nfb.org/images/nfb/publications/bm/bm01/bm0110/bm011007.htm. Although pricing and model information are now outdated, the suggested questions to ask vendors are still on target, and information on current models is included at Abledata.com. Most embossers still use specialized pin-feed paper, which is significantly more expensive than standard paper, at around $37 per ream. (After you remove the pin-feed strips, don't throw them out; they make irresistible cat toys.)

Embosser printing is quite loud, so you will want to either put it in an out-of-the-way area or use an acoustic hood. Ask the embosser vendor if it has a hood to recommend, or find a contractor to construct something custom.

Braille translation software is available for both Windows and Mac. The cost depends on the complexity of what you need to print. Some basic programs for printing straight-forward text files are free; other are not: Duxbury costs $600 and is an easy-to-use Windows program with advanced features, such as support for a large number of languages and ability to handle math formulas (http://www.duxburysystems.com). The Fred's Head blog has a list of braille translation software at http://www.fredshead.info/2007/03/braille-translation-software.html#.UdAgDJwS1nY.

An alternative strategy, if you do not need immediate results, is to use a braille transcription service. These may charge per hour or per page and have a range of turnaround times. The National Federation of the Blind publishes a list of services at https://nfb.org/braille-transcription-resource-list.

## Other Formats

Check with your accessibility resource people about other formats they may be using. For example, some older individuals might still prefer to receive materials on audio tape. If their format of choice is no longer readily available or would be an undue burden to provide, offer to help them explore acceptable and affordable alternatives, such as MP3s (see p. 30), which can be run on an inexpensive player.

## ⌾ Access to Electronic Formats

In an ideal world, electronic formats would be automatically accessible. Unfortunately, most formats require some attention before they can be used with assistive technologies (see chapter 6) or modified to meet users' needs. This section covers several common formats and the likely accessibility issues with each.

## HTML

HTML, because of its extensive flexibility and excellent accessibility support in web browsers, tends to be the best default format for electronic documents that have complex features, such as tables, forms, mathematical formulas (via MathML), and so on. If you have an important document that you cannot make accessible in any other way, consider converting it to HTML, using any necessary accessibility guidelines for graphics and tables (discussed in chapter 7).

# Microsoft Word

Simple Word documents—one column, no graphics, no tables—generally do not present compatibility problems with assistive technology. However, introduction of any complex formatting or graphics requires some attention.

Several ways in which the accessibility of complex Word documents may be improved are similar to the strategies for web documents, including the following.

*Graphics.* Screen reader technologies cannot interpret pictures, charts, and other graphics in Word documents for blind users; therefore, it is necessary to add a text description. The guidelines for composing these descriptions are the same as for HTML (see chapter 7): keep a balance between being thorough and being succinct.

*Tables.* The concept for making data tables accessible is the same as that for HTML (see chapter 7): label column and row headings so that users will hear information that can help them determine the meaning of the cell's contents. Only one problem: as of this writing, there is no way to label row headings, so you will not be able to provide the same level of access to tables with Word that you can with HTML.

*Headings.* Using heading markup to create a hierarchy helps screen reader users assess a page's structure fairly quickly (see chapter 7). In Word, this is done with existing or modified heading styles that are already built into the style sheet list.

*Fonts.* Follow good practices for legibility: avoid small or fancy fonts, hard-to-read color combinations, and extended use of boldface, italics, or underlining.

While Word for Windows has had the capability to add the accessibility features listed here for some time, the "how to" tends to change with each new version. Therefore, you will need to check the implementation details for the version that you are using. The ability to control some of these features in the Mac product, particularly the graphics labeling, is fairly recent, so if you have a version that is earlier than Word for Mac 2011, you may want to upgrade. The Accessible Digital Office Document Project (http://adod. idrc.ocad.ca/) maintains a website that lists accessible authoring techniques for Word, Excel, PowerPoint, and PDF, covering many versions of these products.

Recent versions of Word have also had a built-in accessibility checker; this is not exhaustive but will catch several common issues. In Word 2010, this can be accessed by going to File → Info → Check for Issues → Check Accessibility. Accessibility checkers in Excel and PowerPoint can be reached via the same path.

# Cloud-Based Word Processors

Google and Microsoft are leading a new rush toward creating online word processors that enhance the ability to edit documents collaboratively. However, the accessibility of these documents has been unpredictable. At this point, the safest bet would be to provide a redundant version of the completed document in Word or HTML. It is usually fairly easy to download and save a copy of these documents in a Word format.

# PDF

PDF remains a tricky format to make genuinely accessible, particularly if you are trying to retrofit a file that is already in PDF format. If you can convert the file to Word or, even better, if you have access to a Word file that was used to generate the PDF, providing this file as an alternative format, editing as necessary (as described on p. 33), is usually the most reliable way to go.

Adobe publishes guidelines on how to make documents accessible using Acrobat or InDesign, but this can be an exasperating process. If you have a Word file and need to generate an accessible PDF, a program called CommonLook Office (formerly called PDF Accessibility Wizard) is helpful, easy to use, and cheaper than buying a full Adobe product. CommonLook Office is a Word plug-in that reviews your document and tells you what needs to be fixed. It can then be used to generate a PDF file with maximized accessibility. Two versions are available: standard, which handles basic documents, and professional, which handles documents that have forms and complex tables. If you only have a few documents to convert, CommonLook does the work for you for a per-page charge, which may prove more cost-effective. CommonLook's website is http://www.commonlook.com. (If you want to try using the accessibility features of Acrobat or In-Design guidelines anyway, a great deal of information is linked from http://www.adobe.com/accessibility/products/acrobat/.)

Adobe Acrobat Reader has features that can attempt to improve the user experience for accessing existing documents that may or may not have been optimized for accessibility. In Reader 11, these are located under Edit → Accessibility and include the following two options.

*Change Reading Options.* This item that lets the user specify how screen readers and text-to-speech programs should try to interpret the document and whether the whole document should be read or just the current page.

*Setup Assistant.* This feature includes the two Change Reading Options settings plus several more options that may make documents work better with speech output and magnification software.

## Online Databases

In 2010 Jennifer Tatomir, a blind student at the University of Michigan School of Information, reviewed thirty-two academic library databases for accessibility, assessing both the structure of the databases and the materials that these databases contained. She found that 72 percent were inaccessible or only marginally accessible and that even those with some accessibility provisions "fail to contain all of the forms and functionalities essential for adaptive technology users to conduct the detailed research integral to academic and professional scholarship" (Tatomir and Durrance 2010, 593).

Several librarians, led by Adina Mulliken from Syracuse University and Debra Riley-Huff from the University of Mississippi, have been instrumental in putting together the Librarians for Universal Accessibility website at http://www.uniaccessig.org. Librarians for Universal Accessibility is a continuation of an Association of Specialized and Cooperative Library Agencies website that tracked accessibility issues with specific databases (http://ascla.ala.org/toolkit/index.php?title=Accessibility_to_Library_Databases_and_Other_Online_Library_Resources_for_People_with_Disabilities), and it is being developed as a "community place to talk about and review library resources."

Until Librarians for Universal Accessibility is successful in persuading database developers to improve the accessibility of their offerings, it may be necessary for librarians to retrieve files for users. In most cases, this should not be an undue burden; however, if a public library patron has an unusually large number of requests, the library might set a limit and provide information about how an outside assistant could retrieve the documents for them.

## E-Text

Electronic text, or e-text, is published in a range of formats. Part of this has to do with market share: Amazon wants to make sure that the books it sells play only on a Kindle and not on competitors' devices; Barnes and Noble wants to keep the Nook format proprietary; and so on. However, there are currently two formats that can be used to maximize e-text accessibility.

*Digital Accessible Information System.* Also known as DAISY, a set of text markup specifications specifically designed to produce "documents suitable for transformation into different universally accessible formats." such as braille and audio (National Information Standards Organization 2013). In 2011, the accessibility features available in the DAISY format were formally incorporated into the international standard for electronic books, EPUB3, developed by the International Digital Publishing Forum. When publishers choose to use EPUB3 rather than proprietary standards, the accessibility of the resulting materials is far more likely.

*National Center for Accessible Media.* The center has published a resource on using iBooks Author software to create accessible publications. The resource can be downloaded for free from https://itunes.apple.com/us/book/creating-accessible-ibooks/id569179589?ls=1.

Even when files are made accessible, the e-reader hardware used to access them may not have accessibility features such as text-to-speech, magnification, or controls that can be operated by people who have dexterity disabilities. You may be aware of the lawsuit brought by the National Federation of the Blind against the Free Library of Philadelphia for loaning inaccessible Nook readers to individuals older than fifty years, including some blind individuals. The out-of-court settlement of the suit included an agreement that "the library will purchase ten accessible e-readers to supplement the devices it has already purchased, and within four years will use only accessible e-reading devices" (Enis and Schwartz 2012).

While there is no optimally accessible e-reader available at this time, the iPad and iPhone come the closest—not only because these devices have built-in accessibility features that work with e-text to varying degrees but also because free apps can often be used to access various e-text formats. As of this writing, these include apps for

*Kindle:* https://itunes.apple.com/us/app/id302584613

*Nook:* http://www.barnesandnoble.com/u/nook-for-ipad-iphone-ipod-touch/379003589

*Kobo:* http://www.kobobooks.com/iphone

Another option is Blio, which is free e-reading software currently available for Windows, Android, and iOS. The Blio website (http://support.blio.com) had contained links about making the software work with screen readers or inexpensive add-in voices to provide speech output and highlighting, but by the time that this book was going to press, the links had disappeared. Some third-party information is available regarding Blio support for the iOS screen reader VoiceOver from the AppleVis website (http://www.applevis.com/apps/ios/books/blio) and for Android screen readers from http://bits.blioreader.com/Support/Accessibility/Toshiba/Blio_Android_Accessibility_User_Guide.htm#_Toc335323462.

Ken Petri of Ohio State University has developed an extensive matrix covering accessibility issues with various e-text formats and some popular e-readers, available online at http://wac.osu.edu/ebook-access-overview/matrix.html.

# ⓖ Access to Multimedia

## DVDs

Deaf individuals have had an up-and-down relationship with movies. While silent movies provided no barriers—other than missing emotional cues suggested by the musical improvisation of an organ player—talkies were problematic. For a long time, most films widely accessible to deaf and hard-of-hearing people were those that had been subtitled to accommodate a mainstream audience in countries that would not understand the film's original language. However, subtitles assume that the audience can hear ambient audio—such as music, animal sounds, machinery, and what Monty Python used to call "rude noises"—and so do not incorporate it. Captioning is a type of subtitling that does include descriptions of nonverbal audio, such as "Why a duck? Why a-no chicken? [Harpo honks his horn frantically]" or "I wish I could quit you [soulful music plays]" or "Great dinner [burp]."

Most DVDs now come with a captioning option that users invoke as a preference on their playback device where possible. If you provide DVD playback stations in your library, you may want to provide instructions on how to turn the captioning on and off. If your current stations cannot show captioning, consider making the capability a priority consideration when the station is upgraded.

Audio description is the equivalent of captioning for blind people. If you remember the old TV show *Mystery Science Theater 3000,* where humans and robots would toss out jokes during breaks in the dialogue of truly awful movies, you have an idea of what audio description is like. However, instead of wisecracks, audio description provides a spoken version of what is going on—for example, "Rick puts his hand under Ilsa's chin and gently lifts it" or "Katie and Michelle hop down the stairs in unison while holding on to the railing." The number of audio-described movies released each year on DVD is much smaller than the number of captioned films, but it continues to increase. The American Council of the Blind maintains a list of available videos and information on how to turn on the audio description, at http://www.acb.org/adp/dvds.html. It also maintains a list of libraries that lend audio-described videos; if you decide to acquire some of these videos for your collection, you can add your library to the list by sending an e-mail to fbrack@acb.org.

## Online Media

In 2012, Netflix settled a lawsuit by agreeing that all its streaming videos would be captioned by 2014 (Mullin 2012). Although the suit focused on the disproportionate number of videos available through Netflix's home delivery service when compared to its streaming service, this suit has implications for other for-fee streaming services that do not have home delivery options, such as Amazon and Hulu (Johnston 2012).

If you are creating your own online media, the National Center for Accessible Media has a wealth of resources available from http://ncam.wgbh.org. This includes guidelines and free downloadable tools that you can use to add captions and audio description to videos. Amara (http://www.amara.org/en/) is another resource with a free option that is easy to use for creating subtitles or transcripts; a paid version permits videos to be crowd-sourced for captioning and for subtitling in multiple languages. For more information about online multimedia, see chapter 7.

## ◎ Key Points

Different media formats are likely to proliferate, and libraries are likely to have a significant role in determining which have staying power and which do not. By remaining aware of accessibility as a consideration in materials selection and letting vendors know that this is something that your library considers important, you will have an opportunity to influence the development and proliferation of formats that will be usable by as many people as possible.

To borrow and access many materials, patrons need to be able to physically enter your library and find a comfortable environment while they are there. Chapter 4 covers architectural and environmental accessibility.

## ◎ References

Albanese, Andrew. 2012. "Google Scanning Is Fair Use Says Judge." *Publishers Weekly*, October 12. http://www.publishersweekly.com/pw/by-topic/digital/copyright/article/54321-in-hathi-trust-ruling-judge-says-google-scanning-is-fair-use.html.

Association of Specialized and Cooperative Library Agencies. 2001. "Why an ALA Disability Policy? Why Now?" http://www.ala.org/ascla/asclaissues/factsheetabout.

Bond, Gwenda. 2011. "Large as Life: Large Print Publishing in 2011." *Publishers Weekly*, April 4. http://www.publishersweekly.com/pw/by-topic/new-titles/adult-announcements/article/46708-large-as-life-large-print-publishing-in-2011.html.

Bookshare. 2013. "Qualifications." https://www.bookshare.org/_/membership/qualifications.

Caswell, Tom, and LeiLani Freund. 2005. *SPEC Kit 288: Scanning Services for Library Users.* Washington, DC: Association of Research Libraries.

Crews, Kenneth. 2012. "Court Rules on HathiTrust and Fair Use." http://copyright.columbia.edu/copyright/2012/10/11/court-rules-on-hathitrust-and-fair-use/.

Dahlin, Robert. 2002. "Large-Print Publishing: A Site for Sore Eyes?" *Publishers Weekly* 249, no. 46. http://www.publishersweekly.com/pw/print/20021118/40852-large-print-publishing-a-site-for-sore-eyes.html.

Enis, Matt, and Meredith Schwartz. 2012. "Free Library of Philadelphia Resolves NOOK Accessibility Lawsuit." *The Digital Shift*, October 25. http://www.thedigitalshift.com/2012/10/hardware-2/free-library-of-philadelphia-resolves-nook-accessibility-lawsuit/.

FindLaw. 2013. "Notes on 2 U.S.C. § 135a: US Code—Notes." http://codes.lp.findlaw.com/uscode/2/5/135a/notes.

Intellectual Property Owners Association. 2013. "Re: WIPO VIP Treaty and Related Patent Law Concerns." http://keionline.org/sites/default/files/2013.4.15IPO_Letter_WIPO_VIP_Treaty.pdf.

irinazey. 2012. "Copyright @ UM (in brief)." THL News Blog. October 25. http://thlibrary.wordpress.com/2012/10/25/copyright-um-in-brief/.

Johnston, Katie. 2012. "Netflix Reaches Deal to End Lawsuit over Closed Captioning of Streamed Movies, TV Shows." Boston.com. October 10. http://www.boston.com/businessup

dates/2012/10/10/netflix-reaches-deal-end-lawsuit-over-closed-captioning-streamed-movies-shows/JkVQPbvy8uuL79zFVeFRNK/story.html.

Mullin, Joe. 2012. "Netflix Settles with Deaf-Rights Group, Agrees to Caption All Videos by 2014." Arstechnica. October 10. http://arstechnica.com/tech-policy/2012/10/netflix-settles-with-deaf-rights-group-agrees-to-caption-all-videos-by-2014/.

National Information Standards Organization. 2013. "'Daisy' Standards." http://www.niso.org/workrooms/daisy.

National Library Service for the Blind and Physically Handicapped. 2010. "NLS Factsheets: Copyright Law Amendment 1996." http://www.loc.gov/nls/reference/factsheets/copyright.html.

Skokie Public Library. 2013. "Printing, Copying, and Scanning Services." http://www.skokie.lib.il.us/s_about/how/Tech_Resources/printing.asp#scanning.

Tatomir, Jennifer, and Joan C. Durrance. 2010. "Overcoming the Information Gap: Measuring the Accessibility of Library Databases to Adaptive Technology Users." *Library Hi Tech* 28, no. 4: 577–94.

University of California–Berkeley. 2013. "Library Book Scanning Process for Users with Print Disabilities—Berkeley Owned Circulating Material." http://www.lib.berkeley.edu/asktico/procedures/library-book-scanning-process-users-print-disabilities-berkeley-owned-circulating-materia.

University of Texas Libraries. 2007. "Fair Use of Copyrighted Materials." http://copyright.lib.utexas.edu/copypol2.html.

U.S. Copyright Office. 2013. "Copyright Law of the United States of America and Related Laws Contained in Title 17 of the United States Code." http://www.copyright.gov/title17/92chap1.html.

#  Resources

## Books in Electronic Formats

### Requiring Payment and/or Proof of Disability

Bookshare. http://www.bookshare.org.
Hathi Trust. http://www.hathitrust.org.
Library e-Book Accessibility Program. https://www.bookshare.org/_/promo/2010/01/overDrive.

### Free Public Access Books

Project Gutenberg. http://www.gutenberg.org/.
Unchained. http://www.pinterest.com/rosefirerising/unchained-finding-free-books/.
University of Pennsylvania. 2013. "The Online Books Page." http://onlinebooks.library.upenn.edu.

## Specialized Optical Character Recognition Software

Kurzweil 1000. http://www.kurzweiledu.com/kurzweil-1000-v13-windows.html.
OpenBook. http://www.freedomscientific.com/products/fs/openbook-product-page.asp.

## Free Resources for Converting Electronic Text to Audio

Text2Speech. http://www.text2speech.org.
vozMe. http://vozme.com/index.php?lang=en.
YAKiToMe! http://www.yakitome.com/tts/text_to_speech.

## Braille Production

### In-House

Abledata.com. "Braille Printer" (search result). http://www.abledata.com/abledata.cfm?page-id=19327&top=11079&deep=2&trail=11054,11073&ksectionid=0.

McCarty, Michael. "Braille Translation Software." Fred's Head (blog). December 29. http://www.fredshead.info/2007/03/braille-translation-software.html#.UdAgDJwS1nY.

Taylor, Anne. 2001. "Choosing Your Braille Embosser." *The Braille Monitor*. October. https://nfb.org/images/nfb/publications/bm/bm01/bm0110/bm011007.htm.

### Transcriptionists

National Federation of the Blind. 2013. "Braille Transcription Resource List." https://nfb.org/braille-transcription-resource-list.

## Making Office and PDF Files Accessible

Accessible Digital Office Document Project. 2010. "Accessibility of Office Documents and Office Applications." http://adod.idrc.ocad.ca/.

Adobe. 2013. "Adobe Acrobat Accessibility." http://www.adobe.com/accessibility/products/acrobat.html.

CommonLook. http://www.commonlook.com.

## E-Book Accessibility

"Blio." 2012. AppleVis (blog). November 18. http://www.applevis.com/apps/ios/books/blio.

Kindle app for iOS devices: https://itunes.apple.com/us/app/id302584613.

K-NFB Reading Technology. 2012. "Accessibility Tips for Screen Reader Users." http://bits.blioreader.com/Support/Accessibility/Toshiba/Blio_Android_Accessibility_User_Guide.htm#_Toc335323462.

Kobo app for iOS devices: http://www.kobobooks.com/iphone.

National Center for Accessible Media. "Creating Accessible iBooks Textbooks with iBooks." https://itunes.apple.com/us/book/creating-accessible-ibooks/id569179589?ls=1.

Nook app for iOS devices: http://www.barnesandnoble.com/u/nook-for-ipad-iphone-ipod-touch/379003589/.

Petri, Ken. 2013. "E-Book Reader Accessibility Comparison Matrix." http://wac.osu.edu/ebook-access-overview/matrix.html.

## Multimedia Accessibility

Amara. http://www.amara.org/en/.

American Council of the Blind. 2013. "The Audio Description Project." http://www.acb.org/adp/dvds.html.

Kovalik, Gail, and Frank Kruppenbacher. 1994. "Libraries and the ADA: Providing Accessible Media to Deaf and Hard-of-Hearing People." *MC Journal: The Journal of Academic Media Librarianship* 2, no. 1: 1–19. http://wings.buffalo.edu/publications/mcjrnl/v2n1/kovalik.html.

National Center for Accessible Media. http://ncam.wgbh.org.

## Miscellaneous

Pass It On Center. 2013. http://www.passitoncenter.org.

University of Texas Libraries. 2007. "Copyright Crash Course." http://copyright.lib.utexas.edu.

# CHAPTER 4

# Architectural and Environmental Accessibility

It cannot be stressed enough how important it is that adaptations for the disabled are carefully calculated and a part of the budget from the beginning. . . . The library cooperated with representatives from the major disability organizations, and they influenced the designs of toilets, ramps—needed because of a height difference between the buildings and within the children's library—the distances between shelves, door openings, staircase markings and button paneling in lifts. (Petterson 2009, 140)

EVEN IN AN ERA OF INTERNET UBIQUITY and funding crises, brick-and-mortar libraries continue to be built from scratch, refurbished, and rebuilt. The ADA is clear about the need to implement accessibility in new buildings or during renovations and to remove barriers whenever possible in buildings that are not being renovated.

Existing guidelines related to the ADA and other legislation include a great deal of quantifiable information about architectural accessibility, since it is pretty easy to provide a measurement of how wide a door should be to let (most) wheelchair users pass through or describe how protruding objects should be placed so that blind individuals do not run into them. What are harder to quantify are environmental considerations, such as the need for quiet space by people with attention-deficit disorder or accommodations for people with chemical sensitivities. Better resources for addressing these types of considerations include user input and the experiences of other libraries and organizations.

This chapter covers discussions of guidelines related to legislation and information about best practices that provide a more holistic view of making the building and environment accessible. It intends to promote a goal of creating accessibility in a way that makes sense for your library and patrons, rather than simply adhering to specifications.

# ⊚ Background on Applicable Guidelines

The development of architectural access guidelines goes back more than fifty years, well before the passing of the ADA. The landmark publications include the following:

- Although the U.S. Access Board has oversight of developing federal architectural guidelines for accessibility, the American National Standards Institute published "Specifications for Making Buildings and Facilities Accessible to, and Usable by, the Physically Handicapped" in 1961.
- As a result of the Architectural Barriers Act, which was passed by Congress in 1968, the American National Standards Institute expanded its standards and published the "Uniform Federal Accessibility Standards" in 1971.
- In 1991, as a result of the passage of the ADA, the U.S. Access Board issued the "Americans with Disability Act Accessibility Guidelines."
- In 2004, a revised "Americans with Disability Act Accessibility Guidelines"— namely, the "ADA and ABA [Architectural Barriers Act] Accessibility Guidelines for Buildings and Facilities"—combined the technical requirements of the guidelines and the "Uniform Federal Accessibility Standards."
- The most current version of the architectural guidelines, which are referenced in this chapter, were issued as the "2010 ADA Standards for Accessible Design" (hereafter referred to as the 2010 standards; Department of Justice 2010). These standards are available online at http://www.ada.gov/regs2010/2010ADAStandards/2010ADAstandards.htm. Guidance on use of these standards is available at http://www.ada.gov/regs2010/2010ADAStandards/Guidance2010ADAstandards.htm.

# ⊚ Navigating the Guideline Topics

The 2010 standards contains three parts: application/administration (chapter 1, separate for ADA and Architectural Barriers Act), scoping (chapter 2, also separate), and technical requirements (chapters 3–10). Reviewing the latter two parts tends to require a lot of cross-referencing, because an item listed in scoping is usually associated with sections in the technical requirements. Many of the technical requirements include further subreferencing to topics in the 2010 standards: chapter 3 ("Building Blocks") or chapter 4 ("Accessible Route").

Unless otherwise noted, references to chapters in the following discussion indicate chapters in the 2010 standards, not in this book. Chapters in this book are indicated with relevant page numbers.

The explanation here provides a summary of 2010 standards topics that are most likely to be relevant to libraries. Summaries of guidelines referenced in a scope section are provided following the applicable section, except for the widely applicable chapters 3 and 4, which have their own summaries (starting on pp. 47 and 49, respectively). Numbers indicate the relevant section within the 2010 standards, and unless otherwise noted, all images in this chapter have been taken from this standards document. The topics covered are as follows:

- Parking
- Stairways
- Drinking fountains
- Kitchens, kitchenettes, and sinks
- Toilet facilities
- Fire alarms
- Signage
- Public telephones
- Assistive listening systems
- Assembly areas
- Storage
- Dining and work surfaces
- Sales and service (relevant to checkout aisles, service counters, and food service)
- Depositories, vending machines, change machines, and mailboxes
- Windows
- Play areas

Other covered topics include golf courses, animal containment areas, and saunas. If you decide to include any of these or other unconventional features in your library, check the 2010 standards for applicable regulations.

This information is intended to provide only an overview. It does not replace consultation with legal experts, such as your city's disability services specialist, and construction experts about what is appropriate for your particular environment.

## Chapter 1: Application/Administration

Chapter 1 presents a great deal of background information, including the document's purpose (101), where the document provides dimensions relevant to children's measurements (102), use of strategies that provide equal or greater accessibility than those described (103), conventions (104), and referenced standards (105). Section 106 introduces definitions, including a glossary (106.5) that provides specific meanings for many terms used throughout the 2010 standards.

## Chapter 2: Scoping

Chapter 2 starts with two sections of general information about compliance for new construction (201) and existing buildings and facilities (202). Section 203 lists several types of areas that are either fully exempt from compliance, including crawlspaces and other limited access areas (203.4), or partially exempt, such as employee work areas (203.9).

Sections 204, 205, and 206 mandate compliance with 307: Protruding Objects (see p. 47), 309: Operable Parts (see p. 49), and chapter 4, "Accessible Routes" (see p. 49). These chapters also provide complex information about compliance exceptions that likely require legal review to see whether and how they apply to your library, such as accessible route exceptions for certain historic buildings.

207: Accessible Means of Egress references the International Building Code, the relevant portions of which are available at the following websites:

*Egress:* http://publiccodes.cyberregs.com/icod/ifc/2000/icod_ifc_2000_10_par044 .htm or http://publiccodes.cyberregs.com/icod/ibc/2006f2/icod_ibc_2006f2_10_sec 007.htm

*Platform lifts:* http://publiccodes.cyberregs.com/icod/ibc/2000/icod_ibc_2000_10_ sec003_par045.htm or http://publiccodes.cyberregs.com/icod/ibc/2009/icod_ibc_ 2009_10_par082.htm

Sections 208 through 243 alternate between covering features commonly provided for most buildings (windows, bathrooms) and listing the compliance requirements of specific entities (shooting ranges, boating facilities). In most cases, the ".1" section of these guidelines simply states that any building providing this item must be compliant with this guideline, so these sections are omitted from discussion in this book unless they provide unique information. Other parts of a given section that provide information not usually relevant to libraries are also omitted here.

*208: Parking Spaces*
- 208.1 states that special-usage parking spaces, such as those for delivery vehicles, are exempt from 208. However, publicly accessed loading zones must be compliant with 503.
  - 503: Passenger Loading Zones provides dimensions for pull-up spaces (503.2), access aisles (503.3), and vertical clearance (503.5). It also mandates compliance with 302: Floor and Ground Surfaces (see p. 47), with the caveat that there should not be a change in level between the pull-up space and the access aisle.
- 208.2 provides information about the minimum number of accessible parking spaces required. It also states that one out of six accessible parking spaces should meet the 502 dimension requirements for vans.
  - 502: Parking Spaces covers dimensions for car and van parking spaces (502.2), access aisles (502.3), and vertical clearance (502.5). 502 also requires compliance with 302: Floor or Ground Surfaces and 703.7.2.1: Signage (see p. 46) and suggests use of wheel stops to keep adjacent routes accessible (502.7).
- 208.3 mandates that accessible parking spaces be located on the "shortest accessible route" between the parking lot and an accessible entrance.

*209: Passenger Loading Zones* also references 503: Passenger Loading Zones. If there is a bus stop near the library, you may wish to talk to your local bus service about its compliance with this section.

*210: Stairways* references compliance with 504 and provides full or partial exemption for aisle stairs in assembly areas, stairs in play components, and renovation of "stairs between levels that are connected by an accessible route."
- 504: Stairways provides information about compliant treads and risers (504.2, 504.3), nosings (the edges of steps; 504.5), and avoiding water accumulation on

stairways "subject to wet conditions." It also indicates the need to comply with 302: Floor or Ground Surfaces and 505.

- 505: Handrails includes extensive information about design and placement.

*211: Drinking Fountains* references compliance with 602 and discusses compliance requirements based on the number of fountains provided.

- 602: Drinking Fountains covers spout height (602.4 and 602.7), spout location in reference to the entire fountain unit (602.5), and water flow to permit use of a cup rather than direct interaction with the fountain (602.6). It also references compliance with several items in chapter 3: clear floor or ground space (305), knee and toe clearance (306), protruding objects (307), and operable parts (309).

*212: Kitchens, Kitchenettes, and Sinks* references compliance with 804 and 606.
- 804: Kitchens and Kitchenettes covers dimensions for wheelchair entry when a cooktop or range is present (804.2). Sinks (804.4) must be compliant with 606: Lavatories and Sinks, and kitchen storage (804.5) is required to be compliant with 811: Storage. 804.6 covers requirements for appliances, including compliance with the chapter 3 items for clear floor or ground space (305), knee and toe clearance (306), and operable parts (309).
  - 606: Lavatories and Sinks is discussed under 213: Toilet Facilities and Bathing Facilities (later).
  - 811: Storage mandates compliance with the chapter 3 items for clear floor or ground space (305), reach ranges (308), and operable parts (309).

*213: Toilet Facilities and Bathing Facilities* references compliance with 603, 604, 605, and 606 for restrooms.
- 603: Toilet and Bathing Rooms provides information about floor clearance (603.2, which includes a reference to 304: Turning Space), mirror height (603.3), and reach range for coat hooks and shelves (603.4, which includes a reference to 308: Reach Ranges).
- 604 covers water closets (rooms containing a single stall) and toilet compartments (one of multiple stalls within a room). It includes measurements for positioning (604.2), clearance (604.3), seat heights (604.4), grab bars (604.5), flush controls (604.6, including a reference to 309: Operable Parts), and toilet paper dispensers (604.7). 604.8 contains information specific to compartments. 604.9 provides alternative specifications for facilities primarily used by children.
  - 604.5 references 609: Grab Bars, which provides further detail on placement of grab bars as well as specifications for bar design.
- 605: Urinals provides information about height and depth (605.2). It also references 305: Clear Floor or Ground Space and 309: Operable Parts, relevant to the flush controls.
- 606: Lavatories and Sinks includes information about mounting height (606.3), the minimum length of time that automatic faucets should stay on (606.4), and the need to wrap exposed hot water pipes and keep undersink surfaces smooth so that wheelchair users will not burn or scrape their legs (606.5). 606 also references 305: Clear Floor or Ground Space and 309: Operable Parts, relevant to faucet handles.

*215: Fire Alarm* addresses the need to have a redundant visible alarm to alert Deaf and hard-of-hearing individuals. It points to 702: Fire Alarm Systems, which in turn references the 1999 or 2002 edition of the National Fire Alarm Code (NFPA 72).

*216: Signs* mandates signage indicating permanent rooms and spaces (216.2), directional signage (216.3), egress (exit) signage (216.4), parking signage (216.5), entrances (216.6), elevators (216.7), toilet rooms (216.8), telecommunication devices for Deaf and hard-of-hearing individuals (TTYs [teletypewriters]) (216.9), assistive listening systems (216.10), and checkout aisles (216.11). Specifications are provided in 703.

- 703: Signs covers specifications for providing both raised lettering (703.2) and braille (703.3), signage installation height and location (703.4), visual characters (703.5), pictograms (703.6), and accessibility symbols (703.7).

*217: Telephones* covers the provision of public telephones, including specifics on mounting height for wheelchair access (217.2), volume control (217.3), and TTYs (217.4 and 217.5). This section is uniquely affected by modern changes in technology; due to the prevalence of mobile devices, public telephones are following the passenger pigeon into obscurity. It is therefore important to note that this guideline does not say that public phones must be provided, only that where they are provided, they must be in compliance with 217 and 704.

- 704: Telephones covers cord length (704.2.4), volume control and amplifiers (704.3), and TTYs (704.4 and 704.5). 704.2 also references 305: Clear Floor or Ground Space, 307: Protruding Objects, and 309: Operable Parts, in reference to controls and location of phone directories.

*219: Assistive Listening Systems* mandates provision of these auditory aids in "each assembly area where audible communication is integral to the use of the space," such as auditoriums. 219.3 provides a chart for determining how many receivers to provide based on the number of total seats. (See chapter 2 for technical information about assistive listening systems.)

- 706: Assistive Listening Systems provides information on receiver jacks (706.2), hearing aid compatibility (706.3), and audio quality (706.4, 706.5, and 706.6).

*221: Assembly Areas* covers the numbers and location of wheelchair seats (221.2), companion seats (221.3), and aisle seats that allow people to transfer out of their mobility device (221.4), in compliance with 802.

- 802: Wheelchair Spaces, Companion Seats, and Designated Aisle Seats includes specifications for wheelchair seating, including area dimensions and line of sight (802.2), proximity and quality of companion seating (803.3), and specifications for aisle seating (803.4). 802.2 also references 302: Floor or Ground Surfaces.

*225: Storage* says that lockers and self-service shelving should be in compliance with 811: Storage.

- 811 indicates that storage areas should be in compliance with 305: Clear Floor or Ground Space, 308: Reach Ranges, and 309: Operable Parts.
- 225.2.2 specifically mentions self-service library shelves. It requires that there be an accessible route to the shelves in compliance with 402: Accessible Routes, but it does not require compliance with the reach range requirements in 308. (For suggestions on how libraries can help patrons reach items on shelves, see p. 52.)

*226: Dining Surfaces and Work Surfaces* requires that 5 percent of spaces "for the consumption of food or drink" and 5 percent of work spaces for both patrons and staff be compliant with 902.

- 902: Dining Surfaces and Work Surfaces provides height measurements for surfaces used by adults (902.3) and children (902.4). 902.2 mandates compliance with 305: Clear Floor or Ground Space and 306: Knee and Toe Clearance.

*227: Sales and Service* indicates the number of checkout aisles (227.2) and service counters (227.3) that need to be compliant with 904. If your library provides a food service, it needs to be compliant with 904; if this service uses self-service shelves, a number of these need to be compliant with 308: Reach Range.

- 904: Check-Out Aisles and Sales and Service Counters provides height specifications for checkout counters (904.3), sales and service counters (904.4), and food service lines (904.5). Any aisles or walking surfaces on the nearby path of travel need to be compliant with 403: Walking Surfaces. 904.4 also requires compliance with 305: Clear Floor or Ground Space and 306: Knee and Toe Clearance.

*228: Depositories, Vending Machines, Change Machines, Mail Boxes, and Fuel Dispensers* indicates the need for compliance with 309: Operable Parts.

- 228.1 specifically mentions library drop boxes as an example of a depository.
- *229: Windows* indicates that any window that can be opened should be compliant with 309: Operable Parts (see p. 49).

*240: Play Areas* covers the number of play components (swings, slides, etc.) that need to be accessible in accordance with 1008.

- 1008: Play Areas cites chapter 4 ("Accessible Routes") and provides details on certain exceptions (1008.2), gives measurements for platforms that allows children to transfer from their mobility device to a play component (1008.3), and provides playground-specific information about turning spaces and clear floor or ground spaces (1008.4) that build on the information in 304 and 305, respectively.

## Chapter 3: Building Blocks

Chapter 3 of the guidelines covers a range of topics with wide applicability within a built environment. Most of these address the needs of people who use mobility devices—wheelchairs, scooters, walkers, and so on—with the exception of 307, which is intended to help blind people avoid walking into obstructions. These sections are frequently cited elsewhere in the 2010 standards. The sections that contain detailed information are as follows.

*302: Floor or Ground Surfaces.* 302 states that "floor and ground surfaces shall be stable, firm, and slip resistant"—beneficial not only for people with mobility disabilities but also for elders and baby boomers, people with wet boots, running kids, and many others. Specific information is given for carpeted areas (302.2) and grates or similar open areas (302.3).

*303: Changes in Level.* Not all floors are perfectly flat, and 303 provides information about acceptable changes in level (0.25-inch maximum) and how to bevel areas that have a difference in level up to 0.5 inches. Areas with a greater difference in level require a ramp; this is covered in 405: Ramps and 406: Curb Ramps.

*304: Turning Space.* Users of mobility devices often require a clear T-shaped path to turn around—moving forward at an angle, backing up, and moving forward at the opposite angle, as shown in the Figure 4.1. 304 covers providing sufficient space for a turning radius, either in a T-shaped space (304.3.2) or in a circular space (304.3.1). This space must comply with both 302: Floor or Ground Surfaces and 306: Knee/Toe Clearance.

*305: Clear Floor or Ground Space.* This guideline covers the provision of enough space for people to reach a destination object, such as a table. 305.3 indicates that this space should be at least 30 × 48 inches, and 305.5 specifies that this space should permit either a forward or parallel approach, as shown in Figure 4.2.

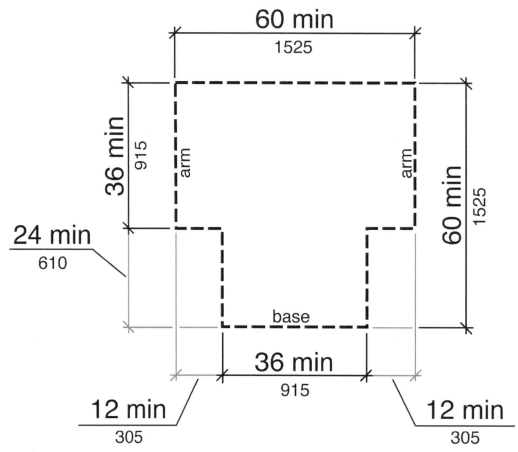

**Figure 4.1.** T-shaped turning space. *Department of Justice (2010)*

305.6 states, "One full unobstructed side of the clear floor or ground space shall adjoin an *accessible* route or adjoin another clear floor or ground space." 305.7 provides guidance specific to alcoves. 305.2 and 305.4 mandate compliance with 302: Floor or Ground Surfaces and 306: Knee/Toe Clearance, respectively.

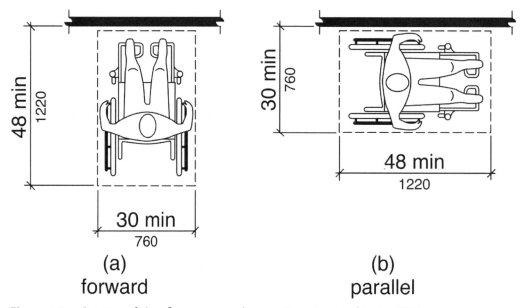

**Figure 4.2.** Position of clear floor or ground space. *Department of Justice (2010)*

*306: Knee and Toe Clearance.* This topic discusses how to ensure that if space under an obstruction is counted as part of the measurements for compliance with 304: Turning Space or 305: Clear Floor or Ground Space, wheelchair users have enough room to ensure that they do not bump their toes (306.2) or knees (306.3).

*307: Protruding Objects.* Regardless of whether blind individuals use a cane or a guide dog to assist with mobility, they still run the risk of running into protruding objects. 307 is designed to minimize the likelihood of such run-ins, whether with attached (307.2) or freestanding (307.3) objects. (Exceptions are made for handrails.) 307.4 covers vertical clearance to reduce the risk of bumped heads. However, 307.5 is a reminder that blind people and wheelchair users may occupy the same space, and modifications made for the former group "shall not reduce the clear width required for *accessible* routes."

*308: Reach Ranges.* People who use mobility devices in a seated position may have difficulty reaching objects such as checkout machines. 308 provides specific measurements that will allow people to reach objects where there is an obstruction (308.2.2) or not (308.2.1), such as a table between the user and the object (see figures 4.3 and 4.4).

Note that the illustrations show that these two specifications are intended for people who use wheelchairs or similar devices where no part of the equipment extends in front of the user. However, devices such as scooters have a "nose" in front that would not allow users to access objects as closely as these illustrations imply, and many wheelchair users have a lap tray or other add-on equipment. 308.3 addresses users of these devices by providing specifications for reaching objects from the side, again with (308.3.2) or without (308.3.1) obstructions (see Figures 4.5 and 4.6). Section 308 also includes some alternative reach ranges relevant to areas where the primary users will be children.

*309: Operable Parts.* This covers items that require or permit user interaction, such as doorknobs. 309.4 states that such items "shall be operable with one hand and shall not require tight grasping, pinching, or twisting of the wrist." (A common way for people without dexterity disabilities to test for 309.4 compliance is to try operating the item with a closed fist.)

309 also sets a 5-pound maximum force requirement for operating the item, which can be tested with a device called a force gauge. Force gauges tend to be $100 and up, so you will probably want to contact your local independent living center or other resource to see if you can borrow one. 309.2 and 309.3 cover compliance with clear floor spaces (305) and reach ranges (308) proximate to operable parts.

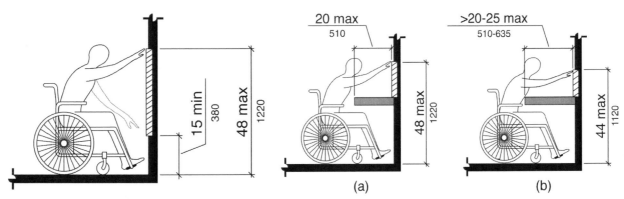

**Figure 4.3.** Unobstructed forward reach. *Department of Justice (2010)*

**Figure 4.4.** Obstructed high forward reach. *Department of Justice (2010)*

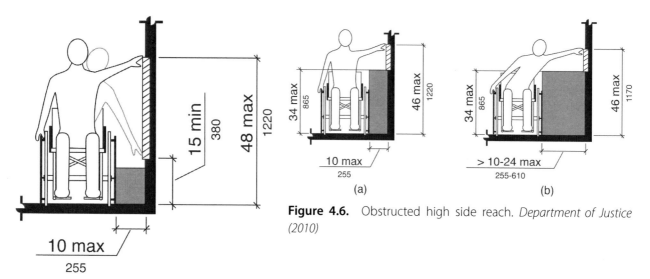

**Figure 4.6.** Obstructed high side reach. *Department of Justice (2010)*

**Figure 4.5.** Unobstructed side reach. *Department of Justice (2010)*

## Chapter 4: Accessible Route

All of the chapter 4 guidelines are dedicated to specifying design features that permit users of wheelchairs, scooters, and so on to travel effectively within a building. These are fairly straightforward and therefore not discussed in detail in this book. The following sections within chapter 4 cover topics of likely relevance to libraries:

402: Accessible Routes

403: Walking Surfaces

404: Doors, Doorways, and Gates

405: Ramps

406: Curb Ramps

407: Elevators

408: Limited-Use/Limited-Application Elevators

410: Platform Lifts

## ⟲ State Regulations

In their book *The Library Renovation, Maintenance, and Construction Handbook*, Donald Barclay and Eric Scott (2011, 65) note, "In addition to abiding by the ADA, several states have enacted their own, more stringent, accessibility standards, and some states have mandated that a percentage of any public funds used for building renovation must be dedicated to improving accessibility." Your state architect's office should be able to provide information about local requirements. If you cannot find its contact information, call your regional ADA center at 800-949-4232 (you will automatically be connected with the center that covers your geographic area). ADA center staff may also be able to provide information themselves. A list of all ADA centers is at http://wdcrobcolp01.ed.gov/Programs/EROD/org_list.cfm?category_cd=DBT.

In addition to your state's guidelines, it may be useful to review those for other states. For example, California's guidelines provide specifics for calculating book stack areas: stack and cross aisles should be at least 36 inches wide; end aisles should be at least 44 inches wide; and freestanding rows of stacks should not exceed 21 feet in length (Barclay and Scott 2011, 77). It is also worth noting that in 2013, California adopted a building code that merged state and federal requirements into a single document, and it is possible that other states may follow (Lamoureux 2013).

## Funding Strategies

There are no extra building costs associated with implementing many accessibility standards, such as installing a water fountain at a compliant height. However, there can be significant costs associated with having to rip out and reinstall noncompliant fountains. This can leave libraries that need to upgrade in a financial quandary. However, there are examples of a variety of funding sources that have allowed libraries to meet or exceed ADA requirements:

- Colusa County (WA) committed $50,000 in 2011 to bring the bathrooms in two county libraries into ADA compliance. A supervisor correctly noted, "As long as we continue to have ADA issues, we will never be able to go after federal money" (Meeker 2011).
- The director of the Barney Library (Farmington, CT) surveyed patrons in 2003 and found clear support for renovating the existing building rather than constructing a new one. This renovation included installation of an elevator and ADA-compliant staircase to provide alternatives to a steep spiral staircase. Provision of the $3,000 necessary for the entire renovation project was split equally among a state library construction grant, state bonds, and donations (Pionzio 2011).
- The Rockville (CT) library received $250,000 from the state in 2008 toward a $2 million accessibility renovation. This was an initial phase that "the trustees hope to leverage into a successful private fundraising campaign to cover the full cost of the project" (Farrish 2008).
- In 2005, the governor of Hawaii appropriated $461,000 to cover compliance upgrades in three libraries. A library administrator noted that this would not result in full compliance but would provide significant improvements ("Libraries to Improve Accessibility" 2005).
- The Cary Library in Houlton (ME) received $21,000 from a 2004 grant from the Maine Library Commission toward ADA upgrades. The town of Houlton then provided matching funds (Lynds 2004).

## Beyond the 2010 Standards

The 2010 standards primarily cover the needs of people who have difficulty moving from place to place due to ambulatory or visual disabilities, with some attention paid to the communication needs of people who are deaf or hard of hearing. However, some factors not covered by legal mandates still fall under the scope of the library's commitment to providing excellent service to all patrons.

The following topics are not intended to be exhaustive. Check with your accessibility resource people (see chapter 1) for other ideas or areas of concern.

## Symbiosis with Other Design Considerations

> Automatic doors eliminate the need for a special power-assisted door and are a boon not only for people with disabilities but also for anyone carrying a load of books, pushing a stroller, wrangling three or four children, or otherwise not in a good position to manage a manual door. (Barclay and Scott 2011, 76)

When people in the assistive technology field want to make the point that accommodations put into place for individuals with disabilities tend to have much wider benefits, there are any number of examples to cite. Sidewalk curb cuts are mentioned frequently for the reasons that Barclay and Scott indicate. So are captioning decoders built into televisions—equally helpful to people who physically do not hear, people who cannot hear because of ambient noise, and people who want to watch television without disturbing a sleeping partner. A recent example is the word-prediction feature now ubiquitous in smartphones; this has been available for years to help people with spelling difficulties or slow typing speeds.

There are many ways in which standard architectural and environmental features may have a positive impact on accessibility and vice versa. For example, the ADA mandate for a "clear path of travel" when applied to a computer lab would indicate that computer cables and electrical cords be managed properly so that they will not cause a tripping hazard for people who walk with difficulty and so that they will not clash with wheeled devices. This has obvious implications for electronic safety, other ambulatory situations (think running children), and even aesthetics.

There may even be cross-disability benefits. For example, motion-activated towel dispensers have clear implications for people who have physical problems with grasping and pulling. Blogger Brad Feld (2009) realized that they are also ideal for helping him avoid touching publicly used areas in bathrooms so that his obsessive-compulsive disorder does not kick in.

## Reaching Materials

Even though the ability to reach materials on shelves is not covered by the ADA guidelines, library standards of service still dictate that patrons be able to access what they need. Providing signage that lets patrons know that library staff are available to assist them can help address situations where the reach ranges are not accessible.

Some libraries provide grabbers to allow patrons to retrieve items independently. However, as Mary Rumsey (2004, 22) points out, "these plastic grabbers work better with paperbacks; heavy [books] could become dangerous if pulled down from a high shelf." If you are going to provide these, clearly warn patrons about potential hazards.

## Acoustics and Quiet Space

Carol Brown (2002, 122) notes, with admirable understatement, that "libraries are no longer quiet spaces where the staff shush noisy undergraduates or children." This can cause a problem for elders and other people who are hard of hearing. While it is difficult to control ambient noise, it is possible to introduce design features that improve the environment. Janet Wiens (2003, 20) suggests that strategic location of HVAC (heating, ventilation, and air-conditioning) units "as far away from the main library space as possible, preferably in a basement or undergrade" and maximal use of natural and low-voltage lighting will positively affect acoustics.

Brown (2002, 123) also notes that "public, school, and academic libraries are expected to provide areas for quiet study and reading, as well as for computer use." What she does not mention is that as much as quiet is appealing to library patrons at large, it can be essential to individuals with learning disabilities, attention-deficit disorder, and similar types of disabilities. Make sure that your patrons know about your quiet areas and, if necessary, develop policies for priority use of these spaces and/or ensuring that quiet practices are observed.

## Signage

The 2010 standards states, "Characters shall contrast with their background with either light characters on a dark background or dark characters on a light background." In my experience, people with visual disabilities due to natural aging or other causes tend to prefer light text on a dark background; this may also be a preference for people who find too much white space distracting. Check with your accessibility resource people for their input.

The ADA Accessibility Guidelines sections on signage do not mandate braille or tactile lettering for descriptive signage for items such as decorative elements. However, if you decide to make these types of signs accessible, it is helpful to consult the guidelines and your accessibility resource people to ensure a holistic implementation on issues such as placement. There is a wall in a public library that I once visited that had a lovely braille sign describing a nearby painting—and both the artwork and the signage were behind an imposing velvet cord.

## Awareness of Changing Demographics

As baby boomers age in record numbers and as many elders continue to enjoy active lives well past the traditional retirement age, there will inevitably be an increasing number of guidelines on providing accommodations in public places. Some of these will overlap with the ADA; others will go further. For example, the New York Academy of Medicine (2013) has published guidelines on making businesses "age-friendly," including "Have a place where customers can sit and rest" and "Provide adequate lighting." Libraries may also provide assistive technologies that help with access to the building; for example, seven branches of the Alameda Public Library provide inexpensive rollators (wheeled walking aids with baskets for carrying items to the circulation desk) that have proven very popular among users (Alameda County Library, 2001).

## Accommodating Environmental Illness/Multiple Chemical Sensitivity

Environmental illness/multiple chemical sensitivity incorporates a range of medical conditions, including asthma (increasingly common in urban areas), results of veterans' chemical exposure, and immunological diseases. In 1996, the California Senate Subcommittee on the Rights of the Disabled published a report entitled "Access for People with

Environmental Illness/Multiple Chemical Sensitivity and Other Related Conditions" (http://www.ehnca.org/www/books/eimcsf1.htm). It noted that "thousands of people suffer a wide variety of symptoms which can incapacitate them; prevent their access to public places because of indoor air pollution or contact with products which cause the symptoms," and it listed eighteen common barriers to access. Some of these barriers are unlikely to be present in libraries (e.g., cigarette smoke); some are transient (e.g., off-gassing from new carpet); some are under the library's control (e.g., fluorescent lighting and use of cleaning supplies); and some are introduced by library visitors (e.g., perfume).

There is not an easy solution to making your library fully accessible to people with environmental illness/multiple chemical sensitivity, particularly in situations where you may be welcoming people with severe allergies to animal dander and people who rely on service dogs. The 1996 report includes some suggestions, such as using signage for areas that present potential hazards and providing adequate ventilation. The most important thing that you can do, however, is to solicit input and suggestions from accessibility resource people who are affected, or concerned with being affected, by environmental elements. This may include people who have electromagnetic sensitivity and may report effects from being around computers and other sources of electricity.

However, there are some steps that can be taken with little effort that provide a more accommodating environment and demonstrate good faith. Common suggestions include the following:

- Use scent-free soaps in the bathrooms and nontoxic cleaning products throughout the library. A list of products is available from the Berkeley Zen Center, http://www.berkeleyzencenter.org/fragrance.pdf.
- Develop a policy requesting (not requiring) that library visitors not wear scented products, and post it within the building, on your website, and on announcements for any library events.
- Use HEPA (high-efficiency particulate absorption) filters in your ventilation system, and have your air-conditioner checked regularly.
- Provide warning signs in the library and information on your website whenever you are performing or planning to perform an activity that may trigger reactions, such as repainting.

## Maintaining Accessibility

The 2010 standards are clear about creating spaces without permanent barriers to passage by individuals with disabilities—but what about carelessly strewn garbage or randomly parked library carts?

Courtney Deines-Jones (2007, 129) has designed a nifty checklist for doing a "daily facility walk-through," looking for and addressing problems such as blocked routes, uneven carpeting, and missing or broken equipment. You may want to create your own list highlighting potential hazards and other checkpoints specific to your library's environment.

## ⊚ Things to Consider

### Reality

Architectural accommodations are the most quantifiable items mentioned in this book. It is much easier to determine whether the width of a door is sufficient to accommodate a chair than it is to definitively pronounce a website or a meeting to be fully accessible. Yet even following the guidelines to the letter is not sufficient to guarantee true accessibility. For example, 2010 standards 404.2.3 states, "Door openings shall provide a clear width of 32 inches (815 mm) minimum." However, over one third of the current U.S. population is obese (Centers for Disease Control and Prevention 2013), and some wheelchair users are part of this demographic. Many wheelchair models are 30 inches wide, so a door that is only 32 inches wide may prove insufficient for people to get through without banging their elbows.

Kevin Crook has written a useful article on design that accommodates obese people, targeted to hospitals but easy to use for other types of buildings. The article includes suggested modifications to the ADA regulations, such as a 42-inch door width, and is available at http://www.hammesco.com/obesity_bariatrics_hospital_design.html#.UX-1eEcrLkQs.

There is nothing in the ADA or its guidelines that prevents anyone from exceeding specifications. Use input from your accessibility resource people, any professional consultants you are working with, and even your gut feelings to improve on the minimum requirements.

### Marketing Ploys

I once found myself in a hotel bathroom in Utah in front of an old-fashioned paper towel dispenser with a sticker proudly declaring it "ADA compliant"—a hollow boast, since it had no operable parts and therefore would not have been subject to consideration under the guidelines. There are no rules controlling the ability to sell products as being ADA compliant (or, for that matter, as being ergonomic); therefore, marketers can do as they wish. Be skeptical: ask any vendor what specific regulation its product addresses and how, and, if appropriate, ask whether the vendor can provide references to satisfied existing customers.

### Logic

Did I mention that the Utah towel dispenser was mounted more than 6 feet off the floor? I am 5 feet 4 inches, and I could barely reach it; most wheelchair users would have had no luck at all. The 2010 standards does say, "Locate soap and towel dispensers so that they are conveniently usable by a person at the accessible lavatory," but "convenient" may become a subjective concept. A walk-through of the bathroom with wheelchair users and short-statured persons before the dispenser was mounted would have headed off this problem.

## Human Intervention

Remember that the idea of the ADA and accommodation in general is to provide equity of access, which often can be lined up nicely with standard service practices. In a discussion of the redesign of the Malmö City (Sweden) Library, Gunilla Petterson (2009, 140) and her colleagues weighed how much self-help wayfinding information they should provide that was specifically designed for people with disabilities. They concluded that "almost every new visitor has to ask for guidance when entering for the first time, and guidance was a library priority to staff in the entrance hall, with many persons available to help," so they decided against providing materials above and beyond what is provided to nondisabled people. If this had been an American library, it would have been in compliance with the ADA since all new patrons would have access to library staff intervention.

## Creative Solutions

The following examples show how architectural and environmental design can go beyond guidelines to serve the needs of a variety of people.

First, the *American Libraries* Library Design Showcase highlighted nine libraries or branches that put extra thought into accessibility during renovation (Landgraf, 2012). Exemplary models included

- the Georgetown Public Library (Washington, DC), which used a rebuilding opportunity after a fire to improve its flooring—new furnishings appear to strike a balance between improved lighting and maintaining the original 1930s look; and

**Figure 4.7.** Ramp at Ed Roberts Campus. *Photo by Diane Dew, diane@dianedewphotography.com*

**Figure 4.8.** Fountain at Ed Roberts Campus. *Photo by Diane Dew, diane@dianedewphotography .com*

- the Greenfield (MA) Community College library, which "eliminated a physical and emotional barrier to entry in the form of a 44-step staircase at the main entrance"—the rebuilt library greets users with a patio and elevator access.

Second, the Ed Roberts Campus in Berkeley (CA) was designed to house multiple agencies serving people with disabilities. Among other accessibility features, it has a ceiling maximized to absorb ambient noise, making communication easier for people who are hard of hearing. The central design feature is a long ramp (see Figure 4.7); in addition to the required level landings at the top and bottom, it has landings spaced throughout its length so that people can stop and rest partway through the climb. An attractive fountain on the first floor also provides an auditory navigation cue for blind individuals (see Figure 4.8). The building has been written up in *Metropolis* magazine as an example of both accessible and green design: http://www.metropolismag.com/March-2011/ Mission-Driven/.

Finally, minimizing use of volatile organic compounds in building materials helps to accommodate people with environmental illness/multiple chemical sensitivity as well as improve overall air quality. The Chicago-based initiative Clear Air Counts has published a list of case studies showing ways that low volatile-organic-compound design has been achieved, available at http://www.cleanaircounts.org/morelowvocbuildingmaterials.aspx#cs.

## ⓖ Key Points

Your library may have been built or remodeled before the ADA, when the ADA was first implemented, or after the regulations were modified; it may be awaiting construction;

or it may be experiencing some combination of these scenarios. Your situation is likely to affect your legal compliance requirements. In addition, being aware of feedback from users about the architecture and environment of your building will help you identify the needs of your community so that you can respond accordingly.

Once patrons with disabilities know that they will be accommodated within your physical space, they may want to show up to learn from trainings, attend presentations, or admire exhibits. Information on making these accessible is provided in chapter 5.

# References

Alameda County Library. 2001. "New Help Navigating the Library!" http://www.aclibrary.org/services/adaServices/pdf/Rotating%20Walkers%20at%20Alameda%20County%20Library.pdf.

Barclay, Donald A., and Eric D. Scott. 2011. *The Library Renovation, Maintenance, and Construction Handbook*. New York: Neal-Schuman.

Brown, Carol. 2002. *Interior Design for Libraries: Drawing on Function and Appeal*. Chicago: American Library Association.

Centers for Disease Control and Prevention. 2013. "Obesity and Overweight." http://www.cdc.gov/nchs/fastats/overwt.htm.

Deines-Jones, Courtney. 2007. "Low-Cost/No-Cost Ways to Improve Service Right Now." In *Improving Library Services to People with Disabilities*, edited by Courtney Deines-Jones, 123–45. Oxford, England: Chandos.

Department of Justice. 2010. "2010 ADA Standards for Accessible Design." http://www.ada.gov/regs2010/2010ADAStandards/2010ADAstandards.htm.

Farrish, Kate. 2008. "Grant to Help Library Improve Its Accessibility." *Hartford Courant*, December 5, A13.

Feld, Brad. 2009. "The Public Restroom as HCI Laboratory." MIT Technology Review (blog), May 22. http://www.technologyreview.com/view/413578/the-public-restroom-as-hci-laboratory/.

Lamoureux, Eric. 2013. "New Construction Regulations Enhance Accessibility." January 25. http://search.proquest.com.proxy.lib.umich.edu/docview/1277683580.

Landgraf, Greg. 2012. "Library Design Showcase 2012: Building for Accessibility." http://americanlibrariesmagazine.org/content/library-design-showcase-2012-building-accessibility (page no longer available).

"Libraries to Improve Accessibility." 2005. *Honolulu Advertiser*, March 12, B6.

Lynds, Jen. 2004. "Houlton's Cary Library to Improve Handicap Accessibility." *Bangor Daily News,* July 14, B.

Meeker, Susan. 2011. "Libraries to Get ADA Compliant." *Colusa Sun Herald*, July 5. http://www.colusa-sun-herald.com/articles/county-6833-arbuckle-library.html.

New York Academy of Medicine. 2013. "Age-Friendly Local Business Guidelines." http://www.nyam.org/agefriendlynyc/docs/AFLBI-Guidelines.pdf.

Petterson, Gunilla. 2009. "Malmö City Library, Sweden: Beauty vs. Efficiency—Planning for User and Staff Needs." In *Renewing Our Libraries: Case Studies in Re-planning and Refurbishment*, edited by Michael Dewe, 133–43. Surrey, England: Ashgate.

Pionzio, Melissa. 2011. "Renewed Charm: Barney Library Gets $3 Million Update." *Hartford Courant*, February 23, B6.

Rumsey, Mary. 2002. "Libraries Confront the Challenges of Accommodating Disabled Users." *AALL Spectrum* 6, no. 7: 6, 22–23.

Wiens, Janet. 2003. "How to Achieve Good Library Acoustics." *College Planning and Management* 6, no. 8: 20–21.

# ⓖ Resources

Clean Air Counts. 2008. "More Low-VOC Building Materials." http://www.cleanaircounts.org/morelowvocbuildingmaterials.aspx#cs.

Crook, Kevin. 2013. "Strategies for Accommodating Obese Patients in Acute Care Settings." http://www.hammesco.com/obesity_bariatrics_hospital_design.html#.UnDQFxDLkQt.

Lion, Diana. 2013. "(Partial) List of Products for Chemically Sensitive People and Their Allies/Friends." http://www.berkeleyzencenter.org/fragrance.pdf.

Steen, Karen. 2011. "Mission-Driven." *Metropolis*, March. http://www.metropolismag.com/March-2011/Mission-Driven/.

# ⓖ Other Resources

Cheryl Bryan's *Managing Facilities for Results* (Chicago: American Library Association, 2007) includes a toolkit on Americans with Disability Act compliance.

The Designing Libraries website has links to several resources about accessible design. Although the site is United Kingdom based, much of the information is relevant to Americans. http://www.designinglibraries.org.uk/?PageID=42.

The Northwest ADA Information Center (DBTAC Northwest) has a very useful checklist that can be downloaded from http://www.dbtacnorthwest.org/_public/site/files/Checklists_TitleII_DBTAC_Final.pdf.

William Sannwald's *Checklist of Library Building Design Considerations* (Chicago: American Library Association, 2009) contains a thorough ADA checklist. Be sure to use the latest edition, which as of this writing is the fifth.

# Training and Event Accessibility

---

SPONSORING TRAINING SESSIONS AND EVENTS has become a major service offered by many libraries. For example, during a typical week, the Ann Arbor District Library sponsored a workshop on drawing comics, a showing and discussion of a new documentary film, a ceremony for winners of a young adult short story writing contest, a lecture on living with an impaired sense of smell, and a tree "yarn bombing," in addition to ongoing playgroups, story times, and computer trainings. Meanwhile, the University of Michigan libraries hosted several events related to the opening of a new collection dedicated to the filmmaker Robert Altman, a lecture on copyright law, a poetry slam, and exhibits on topics ranging from nature drawing to reproductive rights to the library's collection of materials about Detroit.

Title II of the ADA, section 35.130, states that "no qualified individual with a disability shall, on the basis of disability, be excluded from participation in or be denied the benefits of the services, programs, or activities of a public entity, or be subjected to discrimination by any public entity" (Department of Justice 2012). Title III, section 36.201, says that "no individual shall be discriminated against on the basis of disability in the full and equal enjoyment of the goods, services, facilities, privileges, advantages, or accommodations of any place of public accommodation by any private entity who owns, leases (or leases to), or operates a place of public accommodation" (Department of Justice 2010). Both these statements are likely to be relevant to any event that a library would provide or host.

Can the exact experience of an event always be communicated to attendees with various types of disabilities? No, but it will likely be useful to talk with your accessibility resource people (see chapter 1) about what experiences they would like to have. For example, I once went to a symphony concert with a blind friend who turned to me as the orchestra was tuning up and asked me to describe what the musicians were wearing. Libraries might use one-on-one volunteers or real-time audio describers (see chapter 2) to bring the same information to blind event attendees if requested.

This chapter discusses a variety of strategies for ensuring that your library event planning incorporates consideration of accessibility. It also touches on the library's responsibility for events that it hosts but does not create.

The information in this chapter assumes that events sponsored by the library will be held there. If you are sponsoring an event that will be held off-site or if your building is still working toward compliance, consider reviewing the North Carolina State University Universal Design Initiative's "Accessible Temporary Events," a thorough guide that covers topics such as modifying a host location's policies and procedures and providing temporary alternatives to key pieces of signage that are hard to read or confusing. The guide can be ordered from http://www.ncsu.edu/ncsu/design/cud/pubs_p/pfacilities.htm.

## ⑥ Accommodation Statements

It is becoming increasingly common for all types of organizations to add information about accessibility to event announcements. There are three types of information that these tend to include: invitations to people with disabilities to request accommodations, requests to all attendees to avoid doing things that might affect accessibility, and warnings about aspects of the event that may pose problems.

## Accommodation Invitation

A statement about accommodation requests should, at a minimum, include two pieces of information: who to contact and how far in advance of the event the request should be made. The City of Columbus (OH) has a good boilerplate that also includes a policy statement:

> It is the policy of the City of Columbus that all City-sponsored public meetings and events are accessible to people with disabilities. If you need assistance in participating in this meeting or event due to a disability as defined under the ADA, please call the City's ADA Coordinator at [number] or e-mail [address] at least three (3) business days prior to the scheduled meeting or event to request an accommodation. (City of Columbus 2013)

You may also wish to put information on your website about making accommodation requests. The Salem (OR) Public Library provides a good example:

> To request an accommodation, alternative format of communication, and/or modification of policies and procedures in order to access and benefit from a Library program, service

and activity, a library patron must submit a request for reasonable accommodation. The Request for Reasonable Accommodation Form is available on the City's website. (Alternative formats for the form are also available upon request.) The request for reasonable accommodation must be submitted at least five business days before the scheduled event. If a patron submits a request for reasonable accommodation less than five business days before the event, but the accommodation can still be made before the event begins, library staff will make good faith efforts to provide the accommodation .For questions on a particular accommodation request or for further information on requesting a reasonable accommodation, please contact the Library ADA Coordinator. (City of Salem 2013)

If the library has found the demand for a particular type of accommodation to be consistent and therefore provides it automatically, this should be noted on event announcements as well (e.g., "CART transcription will be provided"). You may also wish to use one or more of the standard disability access symbols to indicate services that will be provided; these symbols can be downloaded at no charge from http://signsanddisplays. wordpress.com/2011/03/06/disability-access-sign-symbols-for-download/.

## Accommodation Requests to the Public

General accessibility-related information usually covers requests for people to avoid using scented products, which can trigger symptoms for people with environmental sensitivity. The U.S. Access Board (2013) has a simple but clear statement for its board meetings that could easily be adapted by libraries: "Persons attending Board meetings are requested to refrain from using perfume, cologne, and other fragrances for the comfort of other participants." Do not forget to let the people conducting the event know about this request as well.

## Warnings

If the event will have integral facets that might be highly uncomfortable or dangerous for some people, it is a good idea to mention this on the announcement so that people can decide to not attend or to seat themselves where they can avoid allergic or other triggers. This can be presented matter-of-factly, without mention of disability. Example text might include "This performance includes strobe lighting," "The presenter will be accompanied by two dogs," "Loud noises will be part of this performance," or "The ritual being demonstrated will include use of scented smudge sticks." Accessibility resource people may have ideas about other things that they would want to be mentioned.

Where appropriate, you might add other information specific to your library. For example, if wheelchair users have complained about people without disability placards using the accessible spaces in your parking lot during popular events, you might include a statement asking people to respect the parking designations and suggesting alternative parking places. If the library has recently installed new carpeting or been repainted, you might mention that in event announcements to alert people with environmental sensitivities.

## ⓖ Presentation/Lecture Accessibility

To ensure a proactive and consistent approach to accessibility, you may want to use a checklist that will help all planners and presenters who will be using library facilities or resources—whether they are affiliated with the library or not—to ensure that they have optimized event accessibility. Appendix B provides a sample checklist that summarizes the suggestions made in this section, with space to add additional items requested by your patrons.

## Accessibility of the Environment

General environmental accessibility, as discussed in chapter 4, should be an ongoing consideration; for example, accessible paths of travel should be kept clear whenever the library is open, not just when an event is scheduled. However, there are some additional considerations when scheduling and setting up an event:

- Select the presentation space that is closest to accessible bathrooms whenever possible.
- Avoid holding meetings in rooms that have new carpeting, fresh paint, or other recent upgrades that may trigger environmental illness.
- Swarthmore College (2012) has published a succinct guide entitled "Arranging an Accessible Meeting Space." The goal of this guide appears to be application of ADA architectural standards (see chapter 4) within mutable spaces; for example, the guide indicates that chairs should be set up to allow aisles that are at least 36 inches wide and that space should be left to allow wheelchair users to turn around. (Key points from this guide are included in the sample checklist.)
- Schedule staff or volunteers to be available before and during the event to provide wayfinding information and handle simple ad hoc accommodations.
- Figure out where people with service dogs will be able to go if their animal needs to relieve itself or if it becomes upset, and let dog users know this as they come in.
- Casually include accessibility-related information in your housekeeping speech, such as the location of accessible bathrooms.
- Keep in mind that presenters might also be people with disabilities. Include a question about accommodation needs on any standard form that you use to book rooms.

## Accessibility of the Presentation

All audience members will benefit from accommodation of different presentation modes and content clarity. Some tips to consider when developing and practicing your presentation include the following.

First, Naomi Lederer (2005), in her no-nonsense book *Ideas for Librarians Who Teach*, has a chapter on visuals that provides a variety of suggestions for improving overall legibility of your presentation. These include ensuring that any handwriting on black/white boards, easels, and so on can be seen from the back of the lecture room, with 72-point type for PowerPoint headings and 48-point type for body text with left-aligned text and bullets, including only necessary information and keeping fonts simple rather than "cute." Additionally, where possible, it is worthwhile considering using white text on a dark background, since this can be easier to read for many people with low vision, including elders, and it avoids the excessive white space that can be distracting to some people with learning disabilities.

Second, following good microphone etiquette can enhance the ability of people who have less-than-perfect hearing to follow what is going on. A 2004 article in *The*

*Total Communicator* (http://totalcommunicator.com/vol2_3/microphone.html) provides useful tips on how to get the most from microphone use. If there will be any type of audience participation, you will want to either have some type of wireless microphone that can be passed around or make sure that the speaker has been asked to repeat the information.

Third, People First is an international group of organizations that empower people with cognitive disabilities to advocate for themselves. The Milton Keynes branch in England developed a series of tips on making printed materials more accessible. Many of these are also relevant to visual presentations, including use of plain English, placing graphics on the right side, and not capitalizing all letters. The full list is available at http://www.ncddr.org/products/researchexchange/v08n03/3_tips.html.

Fourth, anyone who's gone through public speaker training in the PowerPoint era has probably heard the same refrain: Do not read from the slides. However, this assumes that everyone is able to see and interpret the visual presentation, which may not be the case. Encourage presenters to strike a balance between reading a PowerPoint word for word and assuming that everyone can access its content just by looking at it. Lederer (2005, 90) says, "Fewer lines per slide is always better," with a recommendation of no more than seven lines per slide; a side benefit of this philosophy is that people will need less time to absorb the contents of one slide before you move to the next. Also remember to provide an audio description of other visual events, such as the approximate percentage of hands raised around the room in response to a question (Web Accessibility Initiative 2012).

Fifth, as 24/7 Internet access becomes ubiquitous, you may want to make presentation materials available online ahead of time so that people can either review them before the event or access them redundantly on a portable device while the event is occurring.

Finally, new presentation programs, such as Prezi, have the opportunity to create dazzling special effects, but these can be distracting to many people and, if sustained, may cause people with photosensitive epilepsy to experience seizures. Keep the presentation as simple as possible.

Some attendees may request additional accommodations, such as real-time captioning (CART) or audio description (these are discussed in chapter 2).

## Exhibit Accessibility

In the past, library exhibits were generally confined to glass cases; now, they may include interactive elements, multimedia, and a host of other creative features that both engage the audience and pose potential accessibility issues. The Smithsonian Museum has put together an exceptional guide on making exhibits accessible, which is available online at http://accessible.si.edu/pdf/Smithsonian%20Guidelines%20for%20accessible%20design. pdf. Key concepts in its philosophy, many of which are backed with specific how-to information, include the following:

- Materials must be presented in multiple formats.
- Content must be accessible to people with differing cognitive abilities, as well as people who "have difficulty reading English."
- Interactive elements, such as controls, must be accessible.
- Experiences of people with disabilities should be included as part of the exhibit.

The Smithsonian also set a high bar for accessibility in 2000 when it sponsored a "Disability Rights Movement" exhibit that featured touch-screen kiosks, long before touch screens became ubiquitous. The kiosks featured controls developed by the Trace Center (University of Wisconsin) that allowed navigation of the kiosk by people who could not use the touch screens because of blindness or dexterity impairment; similar controls are currently in use on Amtrak kiosks. The kiosk interface has been archived at http://americanhistory.si.edu/disabilityrights/welcome.html.

## Real-Time Online Events

If you plan to hold real-time events online, be aware that most webinar software poses accessibility problems. Two packages generally considered to be accessible are Blackboard (http://www.blackboard.com/Platforms/Learn/Resources/Accessibility.aspx) and Ideal (http://www.onlineconferencingsystems.com/), but neither of these is free.

Things that can be done to maximize the accessibility of a webinar—and that might be added to your presentation checklist if your library frequently sponsors webinars—include the following:

- Make materials available in accessible formats to attendees as far ahead of time as possible.
- As with in-person events, invite attendees to request accommodations within a reasonable time before the event.
- Most current webinar software has a chat function that allows conversations either among all attendees or among selected individuals. This can be used by a CART typist (see chapter 2) to provide real-time transcription for people who cannot hear what is being said. As videoconferencing evolves, it is also likely that there will be more picture-in-picture options to accommodate American Sign Language interpretation.
- Encourage presenters to provide extended pauses after inviting questions from attendees. Some people may need more time to generate a question using their assistive technology or to formulate the wording to their satisfaction.

If your library decides to put some of its archival materials up on the Internet—a PowerPoint from a lecture, a recording of a training session, and so on—check chapter 3 for guidance on providing transcripts and otherwise maximizing the accessibility of this information.

## Children's Events

In addition to the accommodation strategies listed here for adults, children are likely to have additional needs. Some best practices include the following.

First, the Contra Costa County (CA) library system has won awards recognizing the excellence of its programming for people with various types of disabilities. Most recently, they have started an Inclusive Storytimes program, including staff trainings. Librarian Gina Worsham (2013, personal communication) detailed the most important lessons that they learned:

We learned about using fidget toys/manipulatives during our programs to help children focus on the storytime and not interrupt others around them. Most were hesitant to offer any type of toy thinking it would actually increase the number of disruptions. Within a week after the training, one librarian took this idea and turned it into a craft program for her elementary school book club. Several members of the group have disabilities which make it difficult for them to focus or sit long. They made their own "fidget toys," and the librarian commented that several of the kids enjoyed making them and using them during the program, including that they were actually quite calming.

Shortly after the training, a children's librarian contacted her local schools' Special Day Classes. She was quickly connected with the director of the program who asked her to make a library presentation about our Inclusive Storytimes to all of their teachers.

Immediately after the training, several libraries instituted a visual schedule for all of their storytimes. This way all of the kids know how long it is until the craft or play time.

One librarian began using laminated circles of different colors to delineate where each child would sit. This has much improved behavior during her storytimes.

Second, Carrie Banks (2013, personal communication) from the Brooklyn Public Library describes accommodations provided for children's and teens services:

The Child's Place for Children with Special Needs provides library service to children and teens with disabilities and their families. We offer weekly, drop-in, recreational programs for youth at 5 libraries and informational workshops for adults. Our barrier free programs are offered in English and Spanish at two locations; all workshops for adults are translated into Spanish. In addition, our extensive collection of books, CDs, videos and other material is a great source of information about exceptional parenting.

Our children's and teens programs are designed using multiple intelligences and universal design paradigms so that all children can participate. For example arts and crafts programs will have at least 3 types of scissors, collage materials, and staff willing to scribe if necessary so children who have physical disabilities and/or vision issues can participate. Our Maker programs, which are Lego based, have Lego and Duplos. Tweens work in groups or individually from models or free form with or without adult guidance. Our gardens have gardening beds at at least 4 levels as well as moveable beds. They are designed as sensory gardens, to appeal to all of the far senses. We offer a variety of tools and equipment to fit the child to the task. We often have teen volunteers with disabilities such as blindness, autism, Downs, and [cerebral palsy]. Programs at two of our sites are bilingual English Spanish and we offer [American Sign Language] at another.

We incorporate [assistive technology and augmentative/alternative communication] into programs and have them on hand for patrons. Social Stories are posted on our website http://www.bklynpubliclibrary.org/only-bpl/childs-place. Some of them are available in Spanish and Chinese. We have sensory tools on site such as weighted vests, fidgets, gel pillows, etc. Our toys, musical instruments and other learning tools are selected with a variety of abilities and sensory modalities in mind.

Recently, we conducted 5 focus groups as part of our plan to expand teen services. As a result we are offering the Maker programs, will soon offer Lego robotics and are developing adaptive gaming. We are also developing a Zine program with a juvenile detention facility (whose students have high rates of mental illness and [learning disabilities]).

Finally, in recent years, some theaters have designated specific showings of plays or movies that have been designed to accommodate children with autism, which may also prove friendlier to some kids with other disabilities or without disabilities. The Autism Theater Initiative (2013) website describes modifications that it has found useful:

> The shows are performed in a friendly, supportive environment for an audience of families and friends with children or adults who are diagnosed with an autism spectrum disorder (ASD) or other sensitivity issues. Slight adjustments to the production included reduction of any jarring sounds or strobe lights focused into the audience. In the theatre lobby there were quiet areas and an activity area, staffed with autism specialists, for those who needed to leave their seats during the performance. Downloadable social stories (in Word format), with pictures of the theatres and productions, were available several months in advance of the performances. These are designed to personalize the experience for each attendee with ASD.

## Events for Elders

Suggestions presented so far for improving visual and audio accessibility will, of course, be particularly relevant to the majority of elder attendees, whether for targeted or general programs. Libraries have been particularly important in providing computer training for individuals who did not encounter high technology in their youth; as Barbara Mates (2002) points out: "If libraries hope to reach and maintain the support of [elders], staff will need to develop programming initiatives which will bring older adults into libraries. One logical place to start is with computer training."

The National Institute on Aging has published a set of "quick tips" to making computer training accessible to elders, at http://nihseniorhealth.gov/toolkit/toolkitfiles/pdf/QuickTips.pdf. Many of these are relevant for other types of trainings and indeed for other populations, including the following:

- Cite other types of technologies that the participants already use—CD players, cell phones, and so on—as examples of their ability to master new skills.
- Provide plenty of opportunities for participants to ask for help.
- Offer information that is clear and specific, without condescension.
- Stay focused on goals.
- Reinforce information with repetition and hands-on practice.

It is also important to keep the information relevant to user interests. Many elders will be focused on very specific goals for using computers—communicating with family members, say, or learning how to track their financial portfolio—and may be put off by classes that focus instead on social media or other topics they feel are irrelevant. Find out what your class members are interested in, and use examples of these for illustrating general concepts.

## Trainings for Individuals with Cognitive Disabilities

Poorly thought-out training sessions—incomplete presentation of information, lack of opportunities to practice what is being taught, and so on—provide a less-than-optimal experience for all attendees. However, individuals with cognitive disabilities may have particular difficulty extrapolating the information they need from such sessions. Yet, training methods that attend to the needs of participants with cognitive disabilities are likely to benefit all trainees.

Reynolds, Zupanick, and Dombeck (2013) propose four strategies for modifying trainings so that people with cognitive disabilities are accommodated. The examples used here to illustrate these strategies are based on trainings related to computer use but could be extrapolated to a variety of situations.

First, break down tasks into steps, staying on each step until participants have mastered it. Participants with cognitive disabilities may need smaller steps than those without. *Example:* Mouserobics (http://www.skyways.org/central/mouse/page1.html) does a splendid job of teaching mouse use in steps that anyone can follow. As the tasks get harder, users may be taken back a few steps if they make an error so that they get more practice with problematic concepts, but the program does not "scold" them for their mistake.

Second, avoid lengthy verbal explanations. Instead, provide as many hands-on opportunities as possible. *Example:* Instead of providing a full spoken explanation of how to open a Word file and begin typing, provide one or more simple exercises that let participants experience the process directly.

Third, provide visual aids wherever they would be appropriate. This may be useful not only for the actual lessons but also for helping students chart their progress. *Example:* Accompany a description of how to use a search engine by connecting your computer to a projector and showing each step. *Example:* When evaluating typing software for training use, look for programs that can be used to track accuracy and speed improvement.

Fourth, provide immediate feedback. In particular, associate the feedback with the concept currently being taught. *Example:* Have enough assistants in your class so that they can circulate among all participants and let them know whether they have successfully completed your instructions on how to fill out an online form.

## ⑥ Events with Outside Sponsors

If you rent or offer your library space to events sponsored by outside individuals or organizations ("tenants"), Title III of the ADA holds both you (the "landlord") and the tenants responsible for accommodations. The federally published *ADA Handbook* suggests that

> the landlord would generally be held responsible for making readily achievable changes and providing auxiliary aids in common areas and for modifying policies, practices, or procedures applicable to all tenants, and the tenant would generally be responsible for readily achievable changes, provision of auxiliary aids, and modification of policies within its own place of public accommodation. (U.S. Equal Employment Opportunity Commission and U.S. Department of Justice 1992, III-43)

The National Association of the Deaf (2013) provides a helpful example: "A hotel might assume responsibility for providing physical equipment such as a TDD telephone device or amplified telephones and amplification equipment for presentations, while the tenant sponsoring the conference or event might assume the responsibility for qualified interpreter services." In any case, the ADA is clear that the cost cannot be passed on to participants: "A public accommodation may not impose a surcharge on a particular individual with a disability or any group of individuals with disabilities to cover the costs of measures . . . that are required to provide that individual or group with the nondiscriminatory treatment required by the Act or this part" (Department of Justice 2010).

You may want to work with outside presenters to ensure that their events are optimized for accessibility, consistent with what the library does for its own events. Besides sharing your internal checklists and other materials, you may want to ask questions such as the following:

- Are there elements of your presentation that are likely to cause an allergic reaction (e.g., strong odors, animals)? Does your presentation include unusual lighting (e.g., strobes) or loud noises?
- Have accommodations been requested for your events in the past? How were these handled?
- Can we have copies of your handouts in advance so that we can share them with potential attendees who need them before they attend and so that we can convert them to accessible formats?

## Key Points

As with many accessibility considerations, planning goes a long way in improving the accessibility of library events. This applies whether the event is a presentation or an exhibit, whether the audience is participatory or passive, and whether the target group includes adults, children, or elders. Being aware of and implementing established best practices—and soliciting input from your accessibility resource people—will help make this important service available and enjoyable by as many people as possible.

Computer classes are often among the most popular trainings provided by libraries. However, some patrons who visit your library to attend these classes or to take advantage of your public computers may have difficulty using the equipment without modifications. We explore these modifications in chapter 6.

## References

Access Board. 2013. "Board Policy to Promote Fragrance-Free Environments." http://www.access-board.gov/about/policies/fragrance.htm.

Autism Theater Initiative. 2013. "Autism Theater Initiative." http://www.tdf.org/TDF_ServicePage.aspx?id=128.

City of Columbus. 2013. "Meeting Accommodations: Public Meeting Statement." http://mayor.columbus.gov/ADA/content.aspx?id=16548.

City of Salem. 2013. "About Us: Accessibility Information." http://www.cityofsalem.net/Departments/Library/About%20Us/Pages/default.aspx.

Department of Justice. 2010. "Americans with Disabilities Act Title III Regulations." http://www.ada.gov/regs2010/titleIII_2010/titleIII_2010_regulations.htm.

———. 2012. "Americans with Disabilities Act Title II Regulations." http://www.ada.gov/regs2010/titleII_2010/titleII_2010_regulations.htm.

Lederer, Naomi. 2005. *Ideas for Librarians Who Teach.* Lanham, MD: Scarecrow Press.

Mates, Barbara. 2002. "Targeting the Fastest Growing Patron Group—Seniors." *Library Hi Tech News* 19, no. 9: 15–19.

National Association of the Deaf. 2013. "Access to Events, Conferences, or Meetings." http://www.nad.org/issues/education/other-opportunities/access-to-events.

Reynolds, Tammy, C. E. Zupanick, and Mark Dombeck. 2013. "Effective Teaching Methods for People With Intellectual Disabilities." Mental Health.net, May 21. http://www.mentalhelp. net/poc/view_doc.php?type=doc&id=10365.

Swarthmore College. 2012. "Arranging an Accessible Meeting Space." http://www.swarthmore. edu/physical-access-and-learning-support/arranging-an-accessible-meeting-space.xml.

U.S. Equal Employment Opportunity Commission and U.S. Department of Justice. 1992. *Americans with Disabilities Act Handbook*. Washington, DC: Author.

Web Accessibility Initiative. 2012. "How to Make Presentations Accessible to All." http://www. w3.org/WAI/training/accessible.

## ⓖ Resources

Autism Theater Initiative. 2013. "Autism Theater Initiative." http://www.tdf.org/TDF_ServicePage.aspx?id=128.

Blackboard (webinar software). http://www.blackboard.com/Platforms/Learn/Resources/Accessibility.aspx.

Disability Access Symbols. http://signsanddisplays.wordpress.com/2011/03/06/disability-access-sign-symbols-for-download/.

Ideal (webinar software). http://www.onlineconferencingsystems.com.

Mace, Ronald, Rex Pace, and Leslie Young. 2002. "Accessible Temporary Events." http://www. ncsu.edu/ncsu/design/cud/pubs_p/pfacilities.htm.

Milton Keynes People First. 2003. "Tips on Making Printed Materials More Accessible." *Research Exchange* 8, no. 3. http://www.ncddr.org/products/researchexchange/v08n03/3_tips.html.

National Institute on Aging. "Quick Tips for a Senior Friendly Computer Classroom." http:// nihseniorhealth.gov/toolkit/toolkitfiles/pdf/QuickTips.pdf.

Smithsoniam Accessibility Program. "Smithsonian Guidelines for Accessible Exhibition Design." http://accessible.si.edu/pdf/Smithsonian%20Guidelines%20for%20accessible%20design.pdf.

Smithsonian National Museum of American History. "The Disability Rights Movement Exhibition." http://americanhistory.si.edu/disabilityrights/welcome.html.

Swarthmore College. 2012. "Arranging an Accessible Meeting Space." http://www.swarthmore. edu/physical-access-and-learning-support/arranging-an-accessible-meeting-space.xml.

"When You're Using a Microphone . . ." 2004. *The Total Communicator* 2, no. 3. http://totalcommunicator.com/vol2_3/microphone.html.

# Technology Accessibility

WHILE WAITING AT A BUS STOP, YOU PULL OUT YOUR SMARTPHONE to type a quick e-mail. You touch on the various fields within the composition window to move the focus, realizing that to be much more efficient than using a mouse. As you type, a predictive list of words appears; you smile at the absurdity of some of the options, but you find the word you want, saving yourself several keystrokes. The Send button is a bit small for you to find, so you use a pinching motion to invoke the magnification option and then easily press the enlarged button to post your message.

What you may not realize is that you just used three features that are assistive technology staples. Touch screens have been available for years as an accessibility option for people unable to manipulate a mouse, as well as for people who have difficulty understanding how moving the mouse controls the on-screen cursor. Word prediction has helped many people increase their typing speed or figure out how to spell difficult words, and on-screen magnification has long made reading easier for people with low vision or learning disabilities.

Current technology is primarily designed to provide output visually with some use of audio and to permit input via finger-and-hand movement with some use of speech. Since any user may have limited or no use of one or more of these capabilities, assistive solutions are a way to either augment existing capabilities or provide alternative strategies.

Fortunately, the lag time between the release of mainstream technologies and appropriate accommodations has shortened significantly. In the 1990s, there was over a four-year gap between the release of Windows 3.0 and the availability of the first Windows screen reader that could handle a graphics-based operating system, and in 2001 Apple omitted many longtime accessibility features in the first release of OS X. In contrast, a third-party screen reader was available for Windows 8 within less than three months of its release, and iOS products have included a full-featured screen reader and a significant number of other accessibility features from the beginning.

In addition, there is an increasingly prevalent convergence between assistive technology and features available in products marketed to the mainstream, particularly as the latter follows a trajectory toward miniaturization that has turned us all into two-finger typists and squinters. Many significant contributions have come from developers with an assistive technology background. It is no accident, for example, that Raymond Kurzweil, who is credited with developing the flatbed scanner for converting print into electronic formats, began by designing a machine for blind people that converted text to a speakable form ("A Biography of Ray Kurzweil" 2008). In more recent years, Randy Marsden has been one of the developers of the Swype keyboard now widely used to make text entry easier on virtual keyboards; before that, he was known for providing sophisticated access solutions for people with little or no use of their hands, including the on-screen keyboard that is included in the Windows operating system ("Swype—Company" 2013).

My previous book, *Implementing Cost-Effective Assistive Computer Technology* (Vincent 2012), is intended as a guide to selecting, funding, implementing, and maintaining computer accommodations. However, libraries are also acquiring tablets and e-readers for public use and may choose to offer other devices in the future. This chapter is designed to provide guidance on what accessibility issues and opportunities may occur with any current or future technology that the library is likely to offer, and it suggests accommodation strategies to seek out.

While libraries are not in the business of providing solutions for personal equipment, they may be the only local information resource in some communities. Therefore, information is included for reference on some solutions for technologies that the library is unlikely to provide.

## Legal Considerations

In 1992, Robert R. Williams wrote a series of articles summarizing how high-tech assistive technology was covered in the ADA. In both his Title II and Title III articles (1992a, 1992b), he noted that the Department of Justice, which administers both titles,

> does not view the use of some forms of emerging technology (e.g., voice recognition systems) as auxiliary aids or services needed for effective communication. But it does suggest that these devices might be viewed as a means of making services, programs or activities accessible to, or usable by, individuals with mobility or manual dexterity impairments.

While Williams's guidelines are still applicable, the catch is that there is no specific legal information about what assistive technology should be provided. Nor does the American Library Association (2009) provide official guidance; its document "Purchasing of Accessible Electronic Resources" has a mandate but no specifications.

Regulations are continually changing, and it is easy to get bogged down in details and lose sight of the fact that their real purpose is always, as the ADA says, to eliminate discrimination. To ensure compliance with both the letter and the spirit of the current law, start by implementing and providing documentation for built-in and free/open-source technologies for your public devices, using the links to existing materials found in this chapter. Then check with your accessibility resources to see what local needs can be identified and what additional products should be acquired to ensure genuine technological accessibility.

There may also be state guidelines that provide more specificity. Check with your legal advisor or your regional ADA center for more information and to stay up-to-date if requirements change. A list of regional ADA centers is located at http://adata.org/contact-us.

# Acquiring Assistive Technology for High-Tech Devices

Adaptive technology solutions are available in one of four ways. Examples of all these are discussed in this chapter.

## Built-In

All current operating systems, browsers, and so on have some type of accessibility features or options. These are usually available via a control panel. In current versions of Windows, the relevant control panel is called Ease of Access (documentation is linked from https://www.microsoft.com/enable/guides/); in older versions, it was called Accessibility. The Mac equivalent is called Accessibility in OS 10.8 (Mountain Lion; documentation is linked from http://support.apple.com/kb/PH11384) and Universal Access in older versions of OS X. (Throughout this chapter, the more current name is used to refer to the relevant control panel.) Both Microsoft and Apple do a good job of providing online documentation for their built-in features; a search engine inquiry will bring up the latest information.

## Free/Open Source

A variety of assistive technologies can be downloaded and implemented at no cost. OATsoft (http://www.oatsoft.org) is a splendid resource for open-source computer-based assistive technology.

## Commercial

Abledata (http://www.abledata.com) is a huge free database of assistive technologies of all types, including hardware and software products that can be installed on Windows and Macintosh computers. There is no assistive technology category in the iTunes store, but the free Assistive Technology Blog podcasts (https://itunes.apple.com/us/podcast/assistive-technology-blog/id457416632) highlight new products. Ricki Buchanan's AT Mac blog (http://atmac.org) has not been updated in some time but is a wonderful resource on iOS and Mac assistive technologies. Doing a web search on "android assistive technology apps" brings up several articles on apps for meeting various types of access needs; the eyes-free forum on Google Groups (https://groups.google.com/forum/#!forum/eyes-free) is a lively discussion of Android apps relevant to blind and low-vision users.

Some commercial products have a purchasing option that allows installation on multiple computers via your local area network. If your assistive technology is in high demand, this may be a cost-effective way to go.

## Cloud Based

Some free and commercial assistive technology software is being made available via the cloud. The advantage is that the user does not need to be on a specific machine; the technology can be run from anywhere, often cross-platform. The Global Public Inclusive Interface (http://gpii.net) is an initiative planning to take this even further: the vision is that users will be able to select the assistive software that they wish to use and then be able to run it from computers, smartphones, tablets, kiosks, and any other devices connected to the Internet or an intranet.

# ⓖ General Suggestions for Choosing Accommodations

Contact your accessibility resource people (see chapter 1) to find out as much information as you can about what kinds/types of assistive technology individuals in your community are using. Not only will this help determine the products that people are already likely to know when they come into your library, but it will also identify a pool of individuals who may be able to be tapped to provide training, tips, and other types of support.

Occasionally, issues may be addressed through hardware or software solutions. For example, magnification can be achieved through use of small utilities or full software programs to adjust part or all of the text on the screen or through a hardware screen that fits over the monitor. Software tends to provide more flexibility, while hardware tends to be easier to set up.

A huge benefit that came with the introduction of mobile devices was the vastly increased number of do-it-yourself program developers, many of whom have created assistive technologies (including the late rock legend Lou Reed, creator of the app Lou Zoom, which magnifies contact lists: http://www.loureed.com/louzoom/). The drawback is that these programs may not be well supported and may come and go from online stores rather quickly. Look for apps that have been around for a while and have received positive ratings in the Apple or Android product stores as well as blogs run by professionals and/or users (an online search for "assistive technology blogs" turns up a wealth of resources).

Several products have been released in versions for both Windows and Macintosh computers. Be aware that Mac versions tend to be less feature rich and updated less often. If there is no Mac product that does what you want, it is sometimes possible to use Windows emulator programs, such as Parallels, and run the program from there; try this out before you commit to the solution, since the results may or may not be satisfactory.

Chapter 3 of *Implementing Cost-Effective Assistive Computer Technology* (Vincent 2012) has several tips and worksheets to assist with the selection process for computer-based solutions. These can also be applied to selecting accommodations for other types of equipment.

The discussions in the next sections list not only the technology components that are likely to cause access problems but also some possible solutions. Where possible, existing solutions are listed for Windows, Macintosh, iOS devices (the operating system used for mobile Apple products; e.g., the iPad), and Android devices (another common mobile operating system). In a few cases, there are mentions of solutions available for dedicated e-readers such as the Kindle. Where solutions are not listed, a good first step will be to search Abledata.com for options.

# ⑥ Displays

## Definition

Almost all current technology relies on a visual display interface as a primary means of conveying information and presenting options. For individuals who cannot effectively see the display or comprehend the information that it provides through sight alone, these displays will require modifications or alternatives.

## Access Issue 1

Blind or nearly blind people cannot see visual displays.

### Solution 1: Audio Output

Screen-reader technology uses synthesized speech to read information that is visible to sighted people and some hidden information, such as descriptions of graphics on a website (see chapter 7). It has been around since the days when the primary operating system for personal computers was DOS from IBM. As graphic user interface systems such as Windows 3.0 and the Macintosh were released, there was a concurrent introduction of the mouse as a way to place the cursor on any on-screen target, which requires hand-eye coordination. Screen readers therefore needed to expand their functionality so that they could work with keyboard shortcuts already built into the operating system (e.g., Control–V to paste text) and introduce additional shortcuts for screen reader–specific functions, such as reading from the cursor to the end of a page. With the widespread introduction of portable touch-screen devices, screen readers had to incorporate strategies for permitting access to users who cannot see the element they want to activate. A good video of a user demonstrating how screen readers work on a computer is at http://www.youtube.com/watch?v=o_mvO6EQ0tM. Although the technology being shown is somewhat outdated, the principles are still the same.

According to a survey from WebAIM (2013), JAWS (Freedom Scientific, http://www.freedomscientific.com/products/fs/JAWS-product-page.asp) remains by far the most popular Windows screen reader, and it works with a large number of applications. However, it is expensive at $900 and up. Free open-source screen readers, such as NVDA (NV Access, http://www.nvaccess.org) and System Access to Go (Serotek, http://www.satogo.com/en), are quickly gaining popularity. NVDA uses many of the same commands as JAWS and works with the mainstream applications most likely to be offered by libraries such as Firefox and Word. Another popular commercial screen reader is Window-Eyes, by GW Micro (http://www.gwmicro.com).

Windows screen-reader users tend to be highly loyal, and it is important to consult with your accessibility resource people about what screen reader is most widely used in your area. Until you have a consensus, you will want to at least install NVDA to ensure ADA compliance.

For mobile devices, the issue is much simpler. All current Apple products have a full-featured built-in screen reader called VoiceOver. Gestures that it supports include a "rotor," which can be used for navigation, and the use of different numbers of fingers to perform different functions; for example, swiping down with two fingers is a reading command, while swiping down with three fingers is used for scrolling. VoiceOver can be activated and customized via the Accessibility control panel. Documentation for the Mountain Lion version is at http://help.apple.com/voiceover/info/guide/10.8/English.lproj/index.html and for iOS, at http://www.apple.com/accessibility.

Android has a built-in screen reader called TalkBack; links to documentation are available from https://support.google.com/nexus/7/answer/2926463?hl=en. Several third-party options are also available; these include Darwin Reader, which is promoted as also being appropriate for users with learning disabilities (https://play.google.com/store/apps/details?id=com.ndu.mobile.daisy.full), and Mobile Accessibility (https://play.google.com/store/apps/details?id=es.codefactory.android.app.ma.vocalizereng).

Speech output on e-readers is trickier. Unresolved issues with intellectual property have caused publishers to not always permit text-to-speech compatibility with their e-books. As of this writing, the best bet is to offer iOS devices, which can be used with free apps that emulate common e-readers, such as the Kindle (https://itunes.apple.com/us/app/kindle-read-books-ebooks-magazines/id302584613?mt=8) and the Nook (https://itunes.apple.com/us/app/nook/id373582546?mt=8).

A forthcoming trend may be for companies to develop their own screen readers to work with their products. An example of this is ChromeVox (http://www.chromevox.com), which is Google's free Chrome plug-in specifically for accessing the Chrome browser and Google Apps. A lively discussion of ChromeVox occurs through the axs-chrome-discuss forum, archived at https://groups.google.com/forum/#!forum/axs-chrome-discuss.

## Solution 2: Refreshable Braille Output

Although screen readers can be tremendously helpful, they have limitations when it comes to proofreading, particularly for homonyms and for words that do not sound like they are spelled. In addition, screen readers may badly mangle pronunciations—for example, the surname "Schutte" is inevitably pronounced "Skut." In situations that require high precision,

There were two settlements of complaints in 2012 by the National Federation of the Blind against the Philadelphia Free Library (https://nfb.org/national-federation-blind-applauds-settlement-free-library-philadelphia) and the Sacramento Public Library (http://www.ada.gov/sacramento_ca_settle.htm) over provision of inaccessible Nook e-readers. The settlements indicate only the features of the Nook providing problems for patrons with vision impairments and do not indicate names of products that would assist with amelioration.

such as writing programming code or composing a résumé, braille users may prefer the use of refreshable braille. This is also a useful accommodation for people who do not have sufficient hearing to use a screen reader but who have sufficient tactile sensitivity to use braille.

Refreshable braille devices have "cells" with at least six pins, one for each dot that might make up a braille character. Each pin can move up and down to represent a character that appears on the on-screen line where the cursor is currently located. Some devices have two extra pins to communicate additional information, such as the location of the cursor or whether the character is boldface. The devices have keys for moving the cursor and performing other functions, and some can be used for text input as well as output.

Most screen readers—including VoiceOver (both Mac and iOS versions), JAWS, NVDA, WindowEyes, and Mobile Accessibility—come with drivers that can run a refreshable braille device with your hardware. An online search for "refreshable braille [name of screen reader]" should bring up a list of devices that each screen reader supports.

Refreshable braille devices generally range from 40 to 80 cells in length. The American Foundation for the Blind maintains a list of currently available devices at http://www.afb.org/ProdBrowseCatResults.asp?CatID=43, along with a list of questions to be addressed by the library (e.g., "How large is the actual display?" "Does it fit in your work space?") or your accessibility resources (e.g., "How many braille cells do you need?"). Since these devices will cost at least a few thousand dollars, check with your accessibility resources to see if there is a demand for them and if there are suggestions for or against specific models. Patrons may own portable twenty-character devices that they may wish to hook up to your computers; you will need to check if the screen reader you support will be compatible.

### Solution 3: Haptic Feedback

The word "haptic" comes from the Greek word for "grasping or touching" and has long been explored as a blind access solution. Haptic feedback delivered from a touch-screen device provides vibrations or other tactile sensations to help users orient themselves to the screen or confirm that a button or key has been activated. It is likely to become an important access strategy for blind users, particularly when combined with audio feedback such as the familiar "click" when a key is activated, and it will be the primary way that deaf-blind individuals will be able to use touch-screen technology. It is also reassuring to sighted individuals who are simply used to pressing keys and have difficulty adjusting to virtual keyboards without feedback.

Blind SMS Reader (https://play.google.com/store/apps/details?id=michelepisani. sms.pro.blindsmsreader) is already available; it is an inexpensive program for Android phones that conveys text messages via vibrations that emulate braille or Morse code. Apple is actively submitting patents for haptic capabilities, including one that will replace the physical on-off button on an iPad or iPhone (Patently Apple 2012). A limited amount of haptic feedback is already available in some Windows devices that are set up for compatibility with Windows 8.

## Access Issue 2

The monitor may be hard to see.

People with low vision may have difficulty seeing text on the displays. People with learning or other cognitive disabilities may be able to see the monitors but cannot interpret information if it is presented in only a visual format or only certain types of visual formats (e.g., black text on a white background; small print). People with low vision may also have difficulty seeing computer system elements, such as pointers and icons.

## Solution 1: Display Enhancement for People with Low Vision

Software programs that provide a range of visual modifications to the standard screen are available. These modifications may include some or all of the following.

*Magnification.* For use in a public area such as a library, try to choose programs that provide multiple magnification options, ranging from fractional levels that magnify between one and two times the standard view, providing a small but useful boost for elders, to several times the standard view for people with significant visual disabilities. Computers running these programs should also have larger monitors to maximize the amount of magnified text that can be seen at one time; monitors that are significantly longer than they are tall can be particularly useful.

*Magnification modes.* Modes allow users to determine whether the entire screen is magnified or only portions. Mode options may include a "lens" that can be moved around the screen like a magnifying glass, a split screen so that the monitor is divided horizontally or vertically into magnified and unmagnified areas, and a mode that magnifies only the area where the system focus is currently located, such as the line where the cursor is active.

*Color modification.* Some people find it easier to see color combinations other than black text against a white background. Inversion (white on black) is often useful, as is yellow on black or on medium-to-dark shades of blue.

*Font modification.* Many people with low vision find sans-serif fonts such as Arial easier to read. People with dyslexia and other learning disabilities may find it easier to read fonts such as Open Dyslexic (http://opendyslexic.org), where easily confusable letters such as "b" and "d" look more distinctive than they do in more standard fonts. (Not all magnification programs facilitate font modification, but common application programs, such as word processors and browsers, will have their own font-setting capabilities.)

*Pointer and cursor modification.* Some people may have difficulty keeping track of where the pointer is located (the arrow controlled by moving the mouse) or where the cursor is (the "insertion point" line in word processors and website text fields). Pointer modification generally helps users by providing either an ongoing enhancement to the pointer, such as lines or shapes around the cursor that can be modified in size and opacity, or an on-demand enhancement, such as an animated indicator near the pointer whenever the user presses a particular key. Cursor enhancement may take the form of modifying the cursor size, providing visual enhancements, or modifying the cursor blink rate.

*Simultaneous audio.* The audio in display modification programs can be adjusted to several verbosity levels, ranging from only blocks of text to all system elements (menu, dialog boxes, etc.). Unlike true screen readers, they do not have their own keyboard shortcuts that permit full mouse emulation.

There are hardware magnification screens that can be placed over a monitor, but these have a fixed magnification level and do not include color options or the other types of modifications that software provides. They also tend to smudge easily. Therefore, they are usually not the best choice for public computers.

Windows systems have a Magnifier built into the Ease of Access control panel, and Macs have a Zoom feature included in the Accessibility panel. Under the "Make the computer easier to see" Ease of Access option, Windows provides a "Change the size of text and icons" option to adjust system settings without turning on the Magnifier, as well as a set of High Contrast themes for adjusting system color contrast settings.

Windows systems have a few powerful options for making the pointer and cursor easier to track. In the Mouse control panel, the Pointers tab includes many options for changing the shape, size, and color of pointers and cursors. The Mouse → Pointer Options tab includes settings that allow the pointer speed to be adjusted in response to mouse movement, that snap the pointer to the default button in a dialog box, that provide a pointer "trail" when moved, that hide the pointer when not in use, and that put an animated bull's-eye around the pointer when the Control key is pressed. In the Keyboard → Speed control panel, an option permits the cursor blink rate to be adjusted—faster to make it easier to see for some low-vision users, slower to reduce distraction for other individuals.

The following common browsers have built-in magnification, font, and color modification options that modify or override the default presentation of a web page (see chapter 7 for information on making websites maximally compatible with these options):

- Firefox has a Zoom option under the View menu. Font and color options can be controlled using the Tools menu → Options → Content → Fonts and Colors dialog box.
- Internet Explorer has two magnification options available via the View menu: Zoom, which automatically magnifies the entire page, and Text Size, which proportionately enlarges text on pages that have been coded correctly (see chapter 7). Font and color options are set via the Tools menu → Internet options → Appearance.
- Chrome has a Customize and Control Chrome menu, which looks like three parallel lines at the far right of the Chrome window and contains a Zoom option. Chrome does not have a built-in method of changing fonts or colors, but free extensions fill the gap, such as High Contrast (https://chrome.google.com/webstore/detail/high-contrast/djcfdncoelnlbldjfhinnjlhdjlikmph?hl=en-US) and Stylebot (https://chrome.google.com/webstore/detail/stylebot/oiaejidbmkiecgbjeifoejpgmdaleoha?hl=en-US).
- Safari has a Zoom feature that can enlarge the entire page (choose Zoom In from the View menu or press Command– +) or just the text (choose View → Zoom Text Only and then choose View → Zoom In). To control the font sizes, choose Preferences from the Safari menu, click Advanced, select Never Use Font Sizes Smaller Than, and then choose a font size from the pop-up menu.

The two leading commercially available enhancement programs for Windows are ZoomText (AI Squared, http://www.aisquared.com/products) and MAGic (Freedom Scientific, http://www.freedomscientific.com/products/low-vision/MAGic-screen-magnification-software.asp). ZoomText used to be the clear leader in the field, but in 2012 MAGic came out with a new version that has an easier-to-use interface and more powerful features. AI Squared also has a program called ZoomText Express, a "light" version that has four magnification options (1.25, 1.5, 1.75, 2) and a limited number of mode and color settings; this may be a good solution to provide for elders who need small levels of enhancement with a simple interface that does not seem like a blatant accessibility feature. On the Mac side, AI Squared released ZoomText for Mac in 2012; this is the first commercial program for OS X that approaches the quality of the Windows offerings.

Magnification options that can be set by touch-screen gestures are an inherent part of the operating system for mobile devices. Because the text is very small from the perspective of almost all users, "pinch and spread" gestures are becoming second nature to all mobile users. E-readers may have some zoom features, but to ensure maximum accessibility, the use of e-reader apps on an iOS device is still the safest way to go for now.

### Solution 2: Display Enhancement for People with Learning/Cognitive Disabilities

For some people with learning/cognitive disabilities, the modifications described in the programs for accommodating vision are sufficient. However, their accommodation strategies can be idiosyncratic, and additional features may be necessary to facilitate reading as well as assist with writing and note taking.

"Toolkit" programs provide a range of utilities, which may include magnification, modifications for font (type, color, and size), virtual color filters, layout modification, typing aids (e.g., word prediction; see p. 86), and note-taking aids (e.g., virtual highlighters and the ability to extract highlighted text to a separate document). Popular programs include

*Kurzweil 3000*—available for both Mac and Windows (Kurzweil Educational Systems, http://www.kurzweiledu.com/default.html)

*WYNN*—available for Windows only (http://www.freedomscientific.com/lsg/products/wynn.asp)

*Read & Write Gold*—available for both Mac and Windows (TextHelp, http://www.texthelp.com)

The main difference between Read & Write and the other two programs is that the former has a toolbar that can be used directly with common programs such as word processors and browsers, while Kurzweil and WYNN work within their own proprietary windows. Read & Write also has a tool specifically designed to work with Google Docs (http://www.texthelp.com/North-America/readwriteforgoogle).

Kurzweil was one of the first assistive technology providers to develop a cloud-based solution. Firefly (http://www.kurzweiledu.com/kurzweil-3000–firefly.html) is a scaled-down version of Kurzweil 3000 that will appear whenever a registered user logs in to a standard Windows or Mac browser. A Firefly app for the iPad is also available.

# ⦿ Input: Selection

## Definition

While the mouse has yet to fall out of common use, it has been replaced by the touch screen on portable devices, and Windows 8 was designed to be used primarily with a touch screen. This has been an access boon for many people, since it can be physically and cognitively easier to interact with items by touching the screen directly over them rather than manipulating a pointer in their direction. However, people with little or no use of their hands may have difficulty using either the standard mouse or the touch screen.

Both selection strategies also seem unusable by blind people. While the mouse continues to require alternatives, the highly elegant solutions described in the discussion of screen readers (p. 78) allow blind individuals to not only use but even extol the virtues of touch-screen-based mobile devices.

## Access Issue 1

People with dexterity impairments may not be able to manipulate a mouse or activate a touch screen.

### Solution 1: Mouse and Touch-Screen Alternatives

A range of alternatives to the mouse are available to move the cursor. In rough ascending order of complexity and cost (and, therefore, library appropriateness), these include the following.

*MouseKeys.* A utility called MouseKeys is available on Windows systems in the Ease of Access control panel and on Mac systems in the Accessibility control panel. This utility permits individuals to use the keypad on the right side of full-sized keyboards to move the mouse in any direction and emulate mouse clicks and dragging. If necessary, an external keypad can be purchased from an office supply store for around $20. These are easier to use with keypad-less keyboards than implementing the Function key to use the center alpha keys as a keypad, and they can be positioned to the left or in front of the keyboard as required.

*Keyboard shortcuts.* Keyboard shortcuts built into the Mac and Windows operating systems as well as many applications emulate mouse functions, usually with more precision. For example, pressing Control–P on a Windows machine or Command–P on a Mac will usually bring up the Print dialog without having to maneuver the mouse pointer to an icon or menu. Either do an online search for "keyboard shortcuts [name of operating system]" or "[name of application]" to find a list of shortcuts, or check the help documentation.

*Auto-click software.* Auto-click software eliminates the need to press the mouse button. The user positions the pointer over the desired icon or link, and after an adjustable pause, the program performs a left click. These programs also usually display an on-screen matrix with other types of clicking (right, double, etc.); if the user selects one of these, it will be performed as the next click. Options include DwellClick for Mac (http://pilotmoon.com/dwellclick/) and Dwell Clicker for Windows (http://www.oatsoft.org/Software/dwell-click).

*Mouse alternatives.* Alternative mice, such as trackballs and external track pads, can facilitate or eliminate gripping or allow the cursor to be controlled through finger, palm, or mouth movement (although due to cost and sanitation concerns, the last is not appropriate for libraries). Some alternative mice are available through mainstream stores; Infogrip (http://www.infogrip.com) carries a range of more specialized alternative mice.

*Touch screens.* Touch screens are being built into new Windows laptops and monitors to facilitate compatibility with Windows 8. If you have an older Windows device or a Macintosh, you can retrofit it with a touch screen, such as the Magic Touch (http://www.laureatefamily.com/products/descriptions/harddesc1.html).

*Speech recognition.* Speech recognition software (see p. 90) tends to have commands that can carry out mouse functions. A speech recognition capability built into Windows has a limited number of commands; commercial products such as Dragon NaturallySpeaking have more sophisticated command sets. Macs have a "Speakable Items" capability that can be turned on in the Accessibility control panel, allowing interpretation of spoken commands but not dictation, and AppleScript can add additional commands; for more information, see http://www.dummies.com/how-to/content/command-your-mac-with-mountain-lions-speech-recogn.html.

*Switch scanning software.* Switch scanning software sequentially highlights available options, such as the keys on a virtual keyboard or the different words or symbols in an augmentative communication program. The user presses a key, a mouse button, or a switch to select the desired option. Programs such as ScanBuddy (http://www.boundlessat.com/Switches/Scanning-Software/ScanBuddy) provide scanning capabilities for computers. This is not technology that libraries are usually expected to implement, but if you have a number of patrons with significant physical and/or cognitive disabilities, there may be requests for it. The range of available switches is quite large and is designed to take advantage of whatever the most controllable body movement might be for different individuals; switches are available to accommodate movements such as pounding with a fist, hitting with the side of the head, interrupting a beam of light, or raising eyebrows. Companies such as Enabling Devices (http://enablingdevices.com/catalog) carry a range of switches, but since it is impossible to predict what patrons might need, then it would probably be best for users to bring their own switches, if there is a demand for switch scanning. For mobile touch-screen devices, scanning has been a primary access strategy for people who have no ability to press a touch screen or cannot generate sufficient force to activate an option. Products that interface with mobile devices include the Tecla Shield for iOS (http://komodoopenlab.com/tecla/tecla-for-ios) and the ClickToPhone for Android phones (http://www.broadenedhorizons.com/clicktophone-android-bluetooth-switch-scanning). iOS has switch scanning capabilities built in; a useful summary of information about these capabilities is available at http://www.spectronicsinoz.com/blog/apps-and-mobile-learning/accessibility-and-access/switching-it-up-in-ios-7.

*Head mice.* Head mice usually consist of two parts: an infrared unit that mounts on top of a monitor and a silver dot that the user places on his or her forehead or eyeglasses. When the user moves his or her head, the infrared unit translates that into pointer movement. Head mice are expensive, fragile, and hard on the neck and are therefore not recommended for library purchase.

*Eye gaze.* Eye gaze systems are appropriate for individuals whose only reliable movement is their eyes. Such systems track what the user is looking at, moving and activating the pointer accordingly. Current versions of these systems are expensive and require the user to keep one's head quite still.

## Access Issue 2

People who are blind do not have the hand-eye coordination necessary to use a mouse or touch screen.

Screen readers, as noted, use the keyboard to emulate the mouse as well as the screen, or they use gestures to provide touch-screen access. Some efforts have been made to create a haptic (tactile) mouse, but these have yet to gain commercial viability.

## Access Issue 3

People who have cognitive disabilities or are new to computers may have difficulty understanding the cause and effect between movement of the mouse and that of the pointer.

Touch screens that fit over a computer monitor (see p. 83) have long been a good solution for addressing this need, since they provide a more immediate relationship between an action of pressing the screen and the desired result—the application opens, the cursor moves, and so on. If operating systems similar to Windows 8 become ubiquitous, touch-screen capability will become part of standard computers as well as mobile devices.

MouseKeys, alternative mice, and other solutions for people with dexterity disabilities may help these users as well. The large BIGTrack trackball (http://www.infogrip.com/bigtrack-trackball.html) can be effective for new computer users. It also has benefits for users who may inadvertently move a standard mouse as they are trying to click, since they have to take their hands off the ball to reach the buttons. Pair it with the free Mouse Aerobics tutorial website (http://monroe.lib.mi.us/computer_classes/mouse_exercise/mouse_exercise.htm) and watch many new users become mousing pros in a short period.

# ⊚ Input: Keyboard

## Definition

The core keyboard design—numbers, letters, some special symbols, and basic function keys (e.g., spacebar, tab)—has been around since the days of the typewriter. The layout of the keyboard was originally thought to be created to deliberately slow down typists, since fast typing would tangle the metal keys used to strike the typewriter ribbon against the page. Although there have been other keyboard layouts developed, for the most part no one has noticed that computers and mobile devices do not have metal keys or ribbons, and technology developers have persisted with widespread use of the now-inefficient QWERTY layout.

## Access Issue 1

People with dexterity disabilities may have difficulty activating the keyboard.

### Solution 1: Keyboard Augmentations and Alternatives

As with the mouse, there is a range of options that can facilitate standard keyboard use or provide an alternative. The following are listed in rough ascending order by complexity and cost.

*StickyKeys.* StickyKeys is a utility included in the Windows Ease of Access and Macintosh Accessibility control panels. This utility lets you press multikey combinations such as Shift–[letter] sequentially rather than having to hold the keys down simultaneously, which is a particular benefit to one-handed typists.

*FilterKeys.* FilterKeys (Windows: Ease of Access control panel) or Slow Keys (Macintosh: Accessibility control panel) adjusts or turns off key repeats. This is useful for people with cerebral palsy, Parkinson's, or other conditions that cause unsteady hands.

*Virtual keyboards.* Virtual keyboards are built into both Windows and Mac operating systems, although the Windows product is more sophisticated. These can be operated with a mouse or most mouse alternatives. For mobile devices, of course, the virtual keyboard is the default input method. There are also third-party virtual keyboards. Two that can be extensively customized are REACH for Windows (http://newsite.ahf-net.com/reach) and KeyStrokes for Mac (http://www.assistiveware.com/product/keystrokes).

*Dvorak layouts.* The Dvorak keyboard layout is probably the best-known alternative to the standard QWERTY configuration; it was designed to increase touch-typing efficiency by putting the most commonly used letters (including all vowels) on the home row. Two modified Dvorak layouts have been developed to increase input speed for one-handed typists: one for left-handers and one for right-handers. Both Windows and Macintosh operating systems allow you to change your input strategy to any of the three Dvorak layouts: In Windows, open the Region and Languages control panel, click on the Change Keyboards button, in the resulting window click on the Add button, and scroll down until you see English (United States). Click on the plus sign next to this label, then click on the plus sign next to Keyboard, and choose the Dvorak layout that you want. On a Mac, choose Language & Text from the System Preferences window, click Input Sources, then scroll down until you see the Dvorak options. In addition to the three options listed here, Mac has a Dvorak-QWERTY option that lets you temporarily switch to QWERTY by holding down the Command key.

*Keyboard labels.* The Hooleon Corporation (http://shop.hooleon.com) carries wide range of sturdy keyboard labels, including large print, alternative contrast (e.g., black on yellow), braille, and Dvorak/QWERTY.

*Typing tutorial software.* One-handed typists who are willing to learn strategies for typing efficiently on a standard computer keyboard will have the benefit of not needing to find or carry an alternative keyboard. Typing tutors include One Hand Typing (http://www.aboutonehandtyping.com), which is available as a manual on CD for Macs or Windows computers or as interactive Windows software.

*Keyguards.* Keyguards are plastic frames that cover the spaces between keys, making it easier for people with cerebral palsy, tremors, and so on to hit the key they want. Moisture guards protect the keyboard from liquids and dust and are a useful accommodation for people who drool. Turning Point Technology (http://www.turningpointtechnology.com/KG/KGMGMain.asp) sells keyguards and moisture guards for standard desktop and laptop keyboards and can create custom keyguards. Because the information on touch screens changes rapidly, it is not possible to create a keyguard that will work with the range of mobile applications, but Turning Point has a few keyguards for specific mobile apps, such as ProLoquo2Go, a common augmentative communication program.

*Word prediction.* Word prediction designed for assistive technology users is more sophisticated than the "autocorrect" built into mobile phones that can cause such interesting errors. There are also mainstream apps such as Type-O (https://itunes.apple.com/us/app/typ-o-hd-writing-is-for-everybody!/id372971659?mt=8) and SwiftKey (http://www.swiftkey.net/en). While word prediction programs designed for the assistive technology market tend to emphasize accuracy for typists with cognitive disabilities, they can also enhance speed for typists with dexterity disabilities. Commonly used programs include Co:Writer (http://donjohnston.com/cowriter/#sthash.0FHPoycO.vTjcCqTs.dpbs; also available for iOS devices) and WordQ (http://www.goqsoftware.com).

*Alternative keyboards.* Alternative keyboards, like alternative mice, come in a range of configurations. "Split" keyboards are popular accommodations; they can be separated or angled to provide a more comfortable typing experience. The Kinesis Freestyle (http://www.kinesis-ergo.com/freestyle2_link.htm) is particularly customizable; the two sides can be arranged entirely independent of each other so that, say, someone with severe arthritis in one hand but not the other can arrange the sides to meet the needs of each hand. EnableMart (http://www.enablemart.com/computer-accessibility/keyboards/alternative-keyboards) carries a range of options. Be cautious with keyboards marketed as "ergonomic"; there is no certification required to use that designation, and it can be used as easily for marketing as for genuine accommodation.

*Speech recognition.* Speech recognition has become exponentially more usable over the last decade but still poses problems in the library environment. Along with the issues mentioned in the forthcoming Speech Recognition section, it requires a large amount of RAM to work well—the system requirements listed on manufacturer websites would be fine if speech recognition were not also being used with other RAM-hogging programs, such as Word. It also poses obvious privacy issues for the user and noise issues for others when it is used in a public area. If your library can dedicate a separate room or area to using speech recognition, it may be more feasible to implement.

*High-level strategies.* Switch scanning, head mice, and eye gaze systems (see p. 84) can all be used to activate a virtual keyboard.

## Access Issue 2

People with cognitive disabilities may have difficulty recognizing letters or may be otherwise confused by the standard QWERTY keyboard layout

### Solution 1: Alphabet-Order Keyboards

QWERTY keyboard order has no analogue outside of typing. However, very young Americans are commonly drilled on a song that installs knowledge of alphabetic order. It may make sense to provide a keyboard that uses the same alphabetic order so that people with cognitive disabilities have access to something that is already familiar.

The Intellikeys keyboard (http://www.intellitools.com/intellikeys.html) comes with several large-print interchangeable overlays, including one that is in alphabetical order. Overlays developed by the manufacturer have a bar code that allows them to be slipped in and out of the Intellikeys hardware and be automatically ready for use. It is also possible to develop custom overlays with an easy-to-use program called Overlay Maker (http://www.intellitools.com/overlay-maker.html); the overlay is printed out and laminated, and a program called Overlay Sender that is included with the Intellikeys installation disk is used to let the computer know which custom overlay is being used.

### Solution 2: Coded Keyboards

Keys can be designed to contain elements that cue the user, as in the following examples.

First, the Big Blu Kinderboard (http://www.chestercreek.com/kinderboard1.html) uses key color to distinguish among key types: vowels are violet, consonants are green, numbers are red, punctuation is yellow, and function keys are blue. It is Bluetooth enabled, so it can be used with iOS devices as well as Macs and Windows computers. A cheaper alternative would be to daub different colors of three-dimensional fabric paint (available from any craft store), opaque nail polish, and so forth on a standard keyboard.

Second, Intellikeys layouts that associate or substitute pictures for certain letters can be developed with Overlay Maker. For example, I once worked with a former DJ who had poststroke aphasia; he could not remember letters but had retained a voluminous memory for popular music of the later twentieth century. He decided what band or artist he wanted to associate with each letter—B for Beatles, M for Madonna, and S for Springsteen (fortunately he liked ZZ Top and the punk band X!). By cutting and pasting pictures of each musician from the Internet into an Intellikeys alphabetical-order matrix, it became easier for him to understand what he wanted to type. Overlays to perform standard library functions could be developed in a similar fashion (e.g., to perform catalog searches). Overlays that other users have developed can be downloaded from the Classroom Suite Activity Exchange at http://aex.intellitools.com/search.php (free—but registration is required).

Finally, use of puffy paint, as described in Controls (next section), can also provide cognitive cues. For example, you could draw a large "T" on the tab key if people have difficulty remembering where it is located.

# ⑥ Controls

## Description

There is usually one or more steps necessary to start up electronic devices. E-readers and other devices may also have hardware controls for moving between pages or conducting other functions. For people with dexterity or visual disabilities, these controls may provide barriers before the desired electronic materials are even approached.

## Access Issue 1

People with dexterity disabilities may not be able to activate the On button or other controls on mobile devices.

### Solution 1: Switch Access

Switch access, as discussed in the Input: Selection section, can be used as an alternative for pressing controls. An early example was the PageBot (http://www.orin.com/access/pagebot), which can provide switch access to Kindle e-readers and which includes a mount so that the device can be placed at a comfortable angle for reading. As with other types of switch access, this is something that may be more important for librarians to communicate to users as an available solution than to actually provide within the library environment.

### Solution 2: Human Assistance

Turning on a computer or mobile device usually takes a few seconds of a librarian's time. It is not optimal, but it may be the most practical strategy. Consider providing signs encouraging users to contact library staff for this and similar types of assistance.

## Access Issue 2

Blind people and people with low vision may have difficulty finding or identifying controls, especially when the controls cannot be visually or tactilely distinguished from the rest of the hardware.

## Solution: Puffy Paint

Puffy paint (also known as fabric or three-dimensional paint) is available at any craft store. Daub it on critical controls to make them easier to see and feel—a bright color such as red or red-orange is likely to provide good contrast. You can use the same paint to enhance the tactile indicators that most keyboards already provide on the F and J computer keyboard keys.

# ⊚ Audio

## Description

Audio is not always an integral part of computer use—but when it is, it is often critical. Podcasts and multimedia are often used as a way of conveying information, and system beeps can be used as the only default way of indicating that an error has occurred.

There is not yet an effective, broadly usable tool analogous to a screen reader that people with little or no hearing can use to get quick and accurate transcriptions of audio in real time. Perhaps large numbers of aging baby boomers and younger individuals with hearing loss due to rock concerts, Walkmans, and MP3 players will drive the development of such a tool. In the meantime, if you have developed content where audio is a primary component, captioning or a transcript will be necessary. (For information about captioned DVDs and other prerecorded audio, see chapter 3.)

## Access Issue 1

People who are deaf or hard of hearing will not be able to access spoken information.

## Access Issue 2

People with learning/cognitive disabilities who require multimodal access to text will have difficulty with audio-only presentation, just as they have difficulty with visual-only presentation.

### Solution 1: Automatic Transcription

Automatic transcription works in the same way as speech input: it parses audio and turns it into equivalent text. As of this writing, automatic transcription is highly unreliable and does not provide a satisfactory solution in situations where it is important to have a reasonably accurate text equivalent. For example, the system that my workplace uses to transcribe voice mail turned my colleague Jim Sullivan into "gym solitaire," and when a kind coworker said that he had "dropped off the ergo keyboards," I was informed that he had "dropped off for a beer." This is extremely funny if you know the context of the call and if English (rather than, say, American Sign Language) is your native tongue; otherwise, not so much. A good discussion, with examples, of why automatic transcription is problematic is available at http://wac.osu.edu/captioning_project/transcription.html.

## Solution 2: Human Transcription

Most captioning is still typed out by humans. While errors can still be introduced, this method tends to have better quality control but still takes time. Mary Reilly has developed a thorough PowerPoint to explain the best ways to create captioned videos, either through for-fee services or on a do-it-yourself basis, that can be downloaded from http:// tinyurl.com/kmplzth. For audio-only materials, such as podcasts, traditional transcription methods are still necessary, although if a script or even outline of the material is available, that can be helpful.

## Access Issue 3

People who are deaf or hard of hearing will not be able to hear system sounds, such as those indicating an error.

## Solution: Redundant Visual Indicators

Built into both the Mac and Windows operating systems are utilities that will flash all or part of the screen when a system alert is issued. The utility is called Sound Sentry in Windows and is available through the "Use text or visual alternatives for sounds" option in the Ease of Access control panel. On the Mac side, the utility name is changed periodically—for Mountain Lion, it is called Screen Flash. Mobile devices may have a flash or vibration option to notify the user of incoming information; check the user documentation or do an Internet search.

# Speech Recognition

## Description

Speech recognition (also known as speech input or voice recognition) is software that transcribes human speech into text or commands for controlling the device on which it is installed. The technology has been evolving since the 1950s, but it is not yet at the level of sophistication depicted in *Star Trek*. It is still fussy about the user's vocal capabilities and environmental issues such as ambient noise. Despite many predictions, it has yet to become a widely used technology on the same level as the touch screen.

For several years, Windows has had a basic built-in speech recognition program available through the Ease of Access control panel. More powerful options are the third-party programs Dragon NaturallySpeaking for Windows (http://www.nuance. com/for-individuals/by-product/dragon-for-pc/index.htm) and Dragon Dictate for Mac (http://www.nuance.com/for-individuals/by-product/dragon-for-mac/index.htm). However, even these will not work for all speakers or for all applications. New limited-function speech recognition tools such as Siri, which is built into iOS devices, are rekindling widespread interest.

If speech recognition does become a dominant input method, it will cause problems for people with no speech capabilities, speech that is hard to understand, or speech that is unsteady—the last group including teenagers (girls as well as boys), going through the inevitable vocal fluctuations of puberty. It is also not an ideal technology for public environments such as libraries, since it needs to be used in a quiet space where ambient noise will not affect accuracy and where users speaking out loud will not disturb other patrons.

Because it is impossible to predict future input and output methods for technology or whether even the current concepts of "input" and "output" will themselves somehow become outmoded, speech recognition is also used here as an example of how to seek solutions for inaccessible elements.

## Access Issue

People cannot use speech recognition as an input strategy due to insufficient vocal capabilities.

## Solution 1: Look for Options Based on Older Technology

There will always be a demand for retroactive input and output strategies, by people with access needs as well as those who simply do not want to learn a new method or who may be in environments where the newer strategy will be less effective. A good current example is hardware keyboards available as an alternative to the virtual keyboards on mobile devices. If speech recognition becomes a dominant input strategy, people will still want keyboards for use in noisy areas, during recuperation from a cold, and for other times when speech recognition is not going to work well.

## Solution 2: Look for New Assistive Strategies

Never underestimate the ingenuity of assistive technology developers. As demand increases, both from end users and from purchasers such as libraries who need to ensure accessibility and compliance, there will inevitably be creative alternatives to dominant paradigms. If speech recognition becomes the default means of controlling one or more types of widely used devices, there will likely be a rise of strategies that might perform functions such as automatically tweaking the audio input for increased accuracy. Because users who do not identify as having disabilities will likely benefit from these strategies as well, as they have from features such as built-in magnification and autocorrect, they are likely to become well documented and continue to be available as new product versions are released.

## Solution 3: Look for Alternative Means of Accomplishing the Same Task

The availability of iOS apps for reading e-text files previously available only via dedicated screen readers is an excellent example of a useful accessibility workaround. Checking or posting questions on reputable forums such as AT-FORUM (subscription information at http://resna.org/membership/waysToGetInvolved/listserves.dot) and QIAT (sign up at http://indicators.knowbility.org/qiat-list.html) will provide access to the latest information.

# ⊚ Key Points

As technology continues to evolve, the need will persist to either provide inherent accessibility features or ensure that enhancements or alternatives are readily available. Traditional technologies (e.g., monitors, keyboards, mice) and evolving technologies (e.g., touch screens, speech recognition) will all have pitfalls for at least one group of users.

Knowing where these accessibility pitfalls may occur and what accommodations to look for can help you be proactive around accessibility issues when acquiring or updating equipment.

Even the best assistive technology, however, will have problems working correctly on the Internet when websites are not coded correctly. Chapter 7 covers accessibility guidelines for creating web pages.

# References

American Library Association. 2009. "Purchasing of Accessible Electronic Resources." http://connect.ala.org/node/79625.

"A Biography of Ray Kurzweil." 2008. http://www.kurzweiltech.com/raybio.html.

Patently Apple (blog). 2012. "New Haptics to Enhance Virtual Keyboards, Replace Home Button." December 20. http://www.patentlyapple.com/patently-apple/2012/12/new-haptics-to-enhance-virtual-keyboards-replace-home-button.html.

"Swype—Company." 2013. http://www.swype.com/footer/company/.

Vincent, Jane. 2012. *Implementing Cost-Effective Assistive Computer Technology*. New York: Neal-Schuman.

WebAIM. 2013. "Screen Reader User Survey #4 Results: Primary Screen Reader." http://webaim.org/projects/screenreadersurvey4/#primary.

Williams, Robert R. 1992a. "ADA & AT: What the Final Regulations Say (Title II)." http://www.resnaprojects.org/nattap/library/atq/adaat2.htm.

———. 1992b. "ADA & AT: What the Final Title III Regulations Say." http://www.resnaprojects.org/nattap/library/atq/adaat3.htm.

# Resources

## Products

Note: Specific products are included as examples, and inclusion on this list does not constitute an endorsement. A more thorough list of options for high-, low-, and no-tech assistive technologies is available via the free online Abledata database, http://www.abledata.com.

## Vision Accommodations

American Foundation for the Blind. 2012. "Refreshable Braille Displays." http://www.afb.org/ProdBrowseCatResults.asp?CatID=43.

Blind SMS Reader screen reader (Android). https://play.google.com/store/apps/details?id=michelepisani.sms.pro.blindsmsreader.

ChromeVox screen reader (Google Chrome browser). http://www.chromevox.com.

Darwin Reader screen reader (Android). https://play.google.com/store/apps/details?id=com.ndu.mobile.daisy.full.

JAWS screen reader (Windows). http://www.freedomscientific.com/products/fs/JAWS-product-page.asp.

Keyboard labels (braille, large print, Dvorak/QWERTY, etc.). http://shop.hooleon.com.

Kindle emulation app (iOS). https://itunes.apple.com/us/app/kindle-read-books-ebooks-magazines/id302584613?mt=8.

Lou Zoom magnification software (iOS). http://www.loureed.com/louzoom/.

MAGic magnification software (Windows). http://www.freedomscientific.com/products/low-vision/MAGic-screen-magnification-software.asp.

Mobile Accessibility screen reader (Android). https://play.google.com/store/apps/details?id=es.codefactory.android.app.ma.vocalizereng.

Nook emulation app (iOS). https://itunes.apple.com/us/app/nook/id373582546?mt=8.

NVDA screen reader (Windows). http://www.nvaccess.org.

Stylebot display modification software (Android). https://chrome.google.com/webstore/detail/stylebot/oiaejidbmkiecgbjeifoejpgmdaleoha?hl=en-US.

System Access to Go screen reader (Windows). http://www.satogo.com/en/.

Window-Eyes screen reader (Windows). http://www.gwmicro.com.

ZoomText and ZoomText Express (Windows), and ZoomText for Mac magnification software. http://www.aisquared.com/products.

## Dexterity Accommodations

"About One Hand Typing" tutorial game (Windows) or training manual (Windows and Mac). http://www.aboutonehandtyping.com.

Big Blu Kinderboard alternative keyboard (Windows and Mac). http://www.chestercreek.com/kinderboard1.html.

BIGtrack trackball (alternative mouse) (Windows and Mac). http://www.infogrip.com/big-track-trackball.html.

Co:Writer word prediction (Windows, Mac, and iOS). http://donjohnston.com/cowriter/#st-hash.0FHPoycO.vTjcCqTs.dpbs.

Dragon Dictate speech recognition software (Mac). http://www.nuance.com/for-individuals/by-product/dragon-for-mac/index.htm.

Dragon NaturallySpeaking speech recognition software (Windows). http://www.nuance.com/for-individuals/by-product/dragon-for-pc/index.htm.

Dwell Clicker mouse emulation software (Windows). http://www.oatsoft.org/Software/dwell-click.

DwellClick mouse emulation software (Mac). http://pilotmoon.com/dwellclick/.

EnableMart (vendor source for many alternative keyboards and mice). http://www.enablemart.com/computer-accessibility/keyboards/alternative-keyboards.

Infogrip (vendor source for many alternative keyboards and mice). http://www.infogrip.com.

Intellikeys configurable keyboard (Windows and Mac). http://www.intellitools.com/intellikeys.html.

KeyStrokes onscreen keyboard (Mac). http://www.assistiveware.com/product/keystrokes.

Kinesis Freestyle adjustable keyboard (Windows and Mac). http://www.kinesis-ergo.com/freestyle2_link.htm.

Magic Touch touch screen (Windows and Mac). http://www.laureatefamily.com/products/descriptions/harddesc1.html.

Mouse Aerobics free online mousing tutorial. http://monroe.lib.mi.us/computer_classes/mouse_exercise/mouse_exercise.htm.

PageBot switch access solution (Kindle). http://www.orin.com/access/pagebot/.

REACH onscreen keyboard (Windows). http://newsite.ahf-net.com/reach/.

SwiftKey word prediction (Android). http://www.swiftkey.net/en/.

Turning Point (keyguards and moisture guards for many types of devices). http://www.turningpointtechnology.com/KG/KGMGMain.asp.

Type-O word prediction (iOS). https://itunes.apple.com/us/app/typ-o-hd-writing-is-for-every-body!/id372971659?mt=8.

WordQ word prediction (Windows and Mac). http://www.goqsoftware.com.

## Learning/Cognitive Accommodations

Firefly reading/writing aid software (cloud-based). http://www.kurzweiledu.com/kurzweil-3000-firefly.html.

Kurzweil 3000 reading/writing aid software (Windows and Mac). http://www.kurzweiledu.com/default.html.

OpenSource dyslexia font. http://opendyslexic.org.

Read & Write Gold and Read & Write for Google Docs (Windows and Mac). http://www.texthelp.com.

WYNN reading/writing aid software (Windows). http://www.freedomscientific.com/lsg/products/wynn.asp.

## Product- and Platform-Specific Documentation and Resources

Apple. 2013a. "OS X Mountain Lion: Use Accessibility Features." http://support.apple.com/kb/PH11384.

———. 2013b. "VoiceOver Getting Started." http://help.apple.com/voiceover/info/guide/10.8/English.lproj/index.html.

Axs-chrome-discuss (forum primarily focused on Google's ChromeVox screen reader for the Chrome browser). https://groups.google.com/forum/#!forum/axs-chrome-discuss.

Cullen, Charlene. 2013. "Switching It Up in iOS 7." Spectronics (blog). September 27. http://www.spectronicsinoz.com/blog/apps-and-mobile-learning/accessibility-and-access/switching-it-up-in-ios-7/.

Intellitools. Classroom Suite Activity Exchange (download site for many Intellkeys overlays). http://aex.intellitools.com/search.php.

LeVitus, Bob. 2013. "Command Your Mac with Mountain Lion's Speech Recognition." http://www.dummies.com/how-to/content/command-your-mac-with-mountain-lions-speech-recogn.html.

Microsoft. 2013. "Microsoft Accessibility: Guides by Impairment." https://www.microsoft.com/enable/guides/.

Nexus. 2013. "Use TalkBack." https://support.google.com/nexus/7/answer/2926463?hl=en.

## Other Information

ADA National Network. 2013. "Contact Us." http://adata.org/contact-us.

American Library Association. 2009. "Purchasing of Accessible Electronic Resources." http://connect.ala.org/node/79625.

Assistive Technology Blog (podcasts). https://itunes.apple.com/us/podcast/assistive-technology-blog/id457416632.

AT-FORUM (general assistive technology forum). http://resna.org/membership/waysToGetInvolved/listserves.dot.

AT Mac (legacy blog). http://atmac.org.

Eyes-Free Forum (forum covering Android apps). https://groups.google.com/forum/#!forum/eyes-free.

Global Public Inclusive Interface (cloud-based assistive technology initiative). http://gpii.net.

OATsoft (list of free open-source assistive technologies). http://www.oatsoft.org.

QIAT (forum covering assistive technology in K–12). http://indicators.knowbility.org/qiat-list.html.

Reilly, Mary. 2013. "Captioning Videos Online." http://tinyurl.com/kmplzth.

Trace Center. 2013. "Introduction to Screen Readers." http://www.youtube.com/watch?v=o_mvO6EQ0tM.

Vincent, Jane. 2012. *Implementing Cost-Effective Assistive Computer Technology*. New York: Neal-Schuman.

# Web Accessibility

Ultimately, providing accessible websites for library users should not be perceived as a hassle. Sure, it may entail a new way of thinking, but the benefits of universal access and improved usability far outweigh the frustration that users may feel when they cannot be self-sufficient in their web-based research. (Fulton 2011, 39)

IN 2009, THE AMERICAN LIBRARY ASSOCIATION PASSED A RESOLUTION urging "all libraries to comply with Section 508 regulations, Web Content Accessibility Guidelines 2.0, or other criteria that become widely accepted as standards of accessibility evolve, so that people with disabilities can effectively use library websites to access information with ease." As this implies, there are multiple sets of guidelines with a tremendous amount of information about web accessibility, and there can be conflicting information about best practices. It can become easy to focus on the details and forget that the real goal of web accessibility is allowing people with disabilities, especially those who use assistive computer technologies (see chapter 6), to access the same online resources as nondisabled individuals.

Just as it is not possible to modify the architecture of a building overnight to make it accessible, it is not a quick task to implement web accessibility. However, if you review your current site, you might be surprised at both how much accessibility is already in place and how many common issues are reasonably easy to fix. You can then plan for an even higher level of accessibility in future developments.

This chapter intends to help you understand the key concepts of web accessibility. It also provides baseline information to help you create ongoing web accessibility practices that are appropriate for your site and your programming resources. Finally, some tips are provided for finding positive models of accessibility features within existing websites and when working with third-party vendors.

# ◎ Web Accessibility Guidelines

For a long time, people have been trying to create guidelines that communicate strategies and procedures for making websites work with assistive technologies and that implement design strategies that will make sites usable for as many people as possible. The most widely used guidelines are discussed here.

## Web Content Accessibility Guidelines 2.0

The Web Content Accessibility Guidelines (WCAG) 2.0 document (http://www .w3.org/TR/WCAG20) was published in late 2008 and replaced WCAG 1.0, which had been implemented in 1999. A major difference between the two versions is that 1.0 was based on the technologies that were available at the time, while 2.0 is based more on principles of accessibility, allowing it to continue being applicable as mainstream technology and web-authoring capabilities evolve. WCAG 2.0 also takes into account changes in the capabilities of user agents (see p. 97). For example, image maps (images that have multiple interactive areas; e.g., a graphic of a bus route that allows you to click on each station to get its address) required redundant text links for accessibility when WCAG 1.0 was published; because user agents can now convey information directly from the image map, this guideline is no longer necessary in WCAG 2.0. A mapping of WCAG 1.0 to 2.0 guidelines is available at http://www.w3.org/WAI/WCAG20/from10/comparison.

WCAG 2.0 is divided into four principles, represented by the acronym POUR:

*Perceivable:* Can the user access all the information on the site?

*Operable:* Can the user navigate to and activate all interactive elements?

*Understandable:* Can the user understand both the information on the page and the page interface (e.g., navigation components)?

*Robust:* Will accessibility be maintained as assistive technologies, browsers, and other user agents change?

Keeping the intent of the four principles represented by the acronym in mind is a good way to maintain focus on the real purpose of the guidelines: ensuring the ability of as many people as possible to use your website.

Each principle has one or more guidelines that provide more concrete information about what the principle means in practice. In turn, each guideline has Success Criteria that are required for conformance and designed to be as testable as possible—"each Success Criterion is written as a statement that will be either true or false when specific Web content is tested against it" (World Wide Web Consortium [W3C] 2008).

Each Success Criterion links to a section on the "How to Meet WCAG 2.0" page (http://www.w3.org/WAI/WCAG20/quickref) that contains links to the following information:

*Sufficient techniques*—specific examples of how to meet the criterion, often including sample snippets of code.

*Advisory techniques*—suggested best practices for providing an enhanced level of compliance. How-to information for most of the advisory techniques has not been described as of this writing.

*Failures*—specific things that automatically cause nonconformance with the criterion.

Each criterion is also assigned one of three conformance levels:

*Level A:* Failure to comply with this criterion means that it will be impossible for one or more categories of users with disabilities to access the page. For example, if a meaningful graphic is provided with no text equivalent (failure to meet Success Criterion 1.1.1), blind users will have no ability to perceive the information contained in the graphic.

*Level AA:* Failure to comply with this criterion means that it will be very difficult for one or more categories of users to access the page. For example, if there is no visible indicator of where the keyboard focus is (failure to meet Success Criterion 2.4.7), it will be cumbersome for sighted nonmouse users to know what will be operated the next time they activate their assistive technology.

*Level AAA:* Failure to comply with this criterion means that there will be complications when one or more categories of users access the page. For example, if a page does not include links to definitions of unusual words (failure to meet Success Criterion 3.1.3), it will be harder for users with cognitive disabilities to understand the page content.

If a page or site meets all Success Criteria at Level A, AA, or AAA, it addresses one of the requirements for conforming to WCAG 2.0 at that level. Other conformance requirements include ensuring that all pages necessary to carry out a process (e.g., searching and retrieving results from an online catalogue) are conformant and that Success Criteria are addressed in a way that will work with assistive technologies. More information is available at http://www.w3.org/TR/UNDERSTANDING-WCAG20/conformance. html#uc-accessibility-support-head.

As the discussion of other guidelines makes clear, WCAG 2.0 is becoming a universal standard. Therefore, this book addresses web accessibility in terms of WCAG 2.0. (A more detailed explanation of WCAG begins on p. 100.)

## User Agents

WCAG makes frequent mention of user agents, which the W3C User Agent working group defines as "any software that retrieves, renders and facilitates end user interaction with Web content, or whose user interface is implemented using Web technologies" (W3C 2011). Browsers and media players are familiar types of user agents. Assistive technology products such as screen readers and speech input software are user agents that usually, but not always, work in conjunction with other agents; for example, there have been browsers designed specifically for blind and low-vision users.

If Ranganathan's second law of library science ("Every reader his/her book"; Wikipedia 2013) was reworded to read "Every web user his/her user agent," a major goal of WCAG 2.0 could be thought of as ensuring this law's enforcement. Regardless of the standard or assistive technology being used, the user would still be able to perceive, operate, and understand any WCAG-compliant page that is of interest to her or him.

## Related Guidelines

The Web Accessibility Initiative, a project of the W3C responsible for WCAG, has also published three related sets of guidelines.

First, the Authoring Tool Accessibility Guidelines (http://www.w3.org/WAI/intro/atag.php) is designed for developers of tools that help people design web pages. Tools designed following these guidelines will facilitate the ability of their users to create WCAG-compliant pages. If you are considering purchase of a web-authoring tool, research or ask the manufacturer about how it aligns with Authoring Tool Accessibility Guidelines standards.

The User Agent Accessibility Guidelines (http://www.w3.org/WAI/intro/uaag.php) is for developers of user agents, which are programs with which users interact to access web pages, e-mail, and so on. (More information about user agents is provided on p. 97.) User Agent Accessibility Guidelines compliance provides accessibility for features that are outside of WCAG's control; for example, WCAG provides specifics about captioning videos, but User Agent Accessibility Guidelines provides information on how the controls on programs used to play back the videos can be made accessible. Research or inquire about how media players or similar agents that you plan to use are compliant with these guidelines.

The Accessible Rich Internet Applications Suite (http://www.w3.org/WAI/intro/aria.php) is a specification that improves the accessibility of dynamic web pages that behave more like applications than like static HTML. The applications can also describe complex controls, such as tabs, expanding menus and text, and other widgets. Last, Accessible Rich Internet Applications landmark roles can easily be employed to describe geographic regions of a page to screen reader users. If your website uses Ajax functionality to carry out functions such as loading search results without refreshing the entire page, talk to your webmasters to ensure that they know about and are using Accessible Rich Internet Applications. Hans Hillen provides useful information and examples of their implementation at http://hanshillen.github.io/jqtest.

## Electronic and Information Technology Accessibility Standards: Section 508

Section 508 was originally added to the federal Rehabilitation Act in 1986 to ensure access to electronic and information technology. Although Section 508 officially applies to federal entities, other organizations have chosen to use Section 508 instead of WCAG as their web accessibility standards. The Section 508 standards are being rewritten to be much closer to WCAG 2.0, but it is not clear when these new standards will be officially published.

Paragraph 1194.22 of the Section 508 standards ("Web-Based Intranet and Internet Information and Applications") consists of sixteen guidelines. Mapping these guidelines to WCAG 2.0 shows that every item in the current Section 508 guidelines is now included in WCAG and that three WCAG Level A guidelines are not included in Section 508. A figure showing the relationship between Section 508 and WCAG level is available at http://www.tomjewett.com/accessibility/508-WCAG2.html.

Other paragraphs of Section 508, which are also being updated, cover the following topics:

1194.21: Software applications that are not web based, including operating systems

1194.23: Telecommunications products

1194.24: Video and multimedia products (televisions and video/multimedia that is not web based)

1194.25: Self-contained, closed products (copiers, fax machines, calculators, etc.)

1194.26: Desktop and portable computer hardware

## International Guidelines

Several countries have created their own versions of web accessibility standards; a list is available at http://www.w3.org/WAI/Policy. In October 2012, WCAG 2.0 was adopted as an international standard by the International Organization for Standardization and the International Electrotechnical Commission (W3C 2012). In 2013, the European Commission (2012) proposed a law to standardize web accessibility practices across all member nations by "defining harmonised requirements" for "certain types of websites of public sector bodies."

## Americans with Disabilities Act

While a variety of guidance documents have been published indicating that the ADA covers website accessibility, to date there has been no set of guidelines specifically associated with ADA compliance. However, in 2010 the Department of Justice released an advanced notice of proposed rulemaking that indicated an intention to add web accessibility requirements to Title II and III. Conventional wisdom indicates that guidelines relevant to these requirements will be based on, if not equal to, WCAG 2.0 (Vu 2013).

## State Legislation

Camilla Fulton's excellent 2011 article "Web Accessibility, Libraries, and the Law" contains a matrix with information about which states have web accessibility statutes that cover libraries, what types of libraries are covered, and where to find state-specific information. Six states (Arizona, California, Florida, Indiana, Kentucky, and Missouri) mention compliance with Section 508 guidelines, while Minnesota mentions WCAG 2.0.

# ⊚ Understanding WCAG 2.0

Web accessibility guidelines generally fall into two types.

## Adding/Modifying Code

The first type involves adding or modifying code so that the page will work with assistive computer technologies. Small coding changes can have major implications. For example, it takes only nine characters of code to put a language attribute at the beginning of a page (Success Criterion 3.1.1). However, this attribute may make the difference to whether a screen reader pronounces words using the rules of the language in which the page is written.

## Designing Page Interfaces for Ease of Use

Accessible web design is often presented as something apart from general usability. In reality, the two are closely related, particularly at the AA and AAA conformance levels. When people first started designing websites, yellow text on a lime green background was a popular color combination. This can be seen as an example of equitable access, since the combination does not meet the WCAG standard for color contrast (Success Criterion 1.4.3) and is not very readable for people without visual disabilities either. Conversely, adherence to accessibility guidelines usually makes pages easier to use for everyone.

## WCAG 2.0 Guidelines

The following information is intended to summarize and clarify the purpose of each WCAG 2.0 guideline. While it is in somewhat technical language, its primary purpose is to allow nonwebsite developers to communicate with those who will ultimately be responsible for implementing accessibility changes. More detailed assistance can be found within WCAG 2.0 itself (http://www.w3.org/TR/WCAG) and the resources at the end of this chapter.

### Perceivable: Guidelines 1.1–1.4

Many of the Perceivable guidelines and Success Criteria are based on an obvious access need: people with visual disabilities will find it hard or impossible to see anything presented in only a visual format, and people who do not hear cannot access sound. In addition, some people with cognitive disabilities have difficulty understanding information presented as words rather than images, or they need to both hear and see text to understand it.

Screen readers and text-to-speech programs (see chapter 6) are very good at reading standard text. (Generally, any text that you can highlight, copy to a word processor, and edit is standard text.) But when they encounter graphic elements—photos, buttons, pie charts, graphics that include bitmapped text—these assistive technologies may either skip over them or read information such as the name of the file used to create the graphic, which seldom proves helpful. *Guideline 1.1* and its single Success Criterion provide guidance on how to add text equivalents that describe enough information about each graphic to convey an appropriate level of information.

Meeting the letter of Guideline 1.1 by adding a text equivalent in HTML (usually via an ALT attribute in an IMG tag) is fairly easy; meeting the spirit is quite another animal. Frequently, text equivalents are either too long—a detailed description of an invisible graphic used as a spacer, for example, which should take a null text equivalent (ALT="")—or they are too short, such as a detailed pie chart with the equivalent ALT="Pie Chart." Dey Alexander, a web design consultant in Melbourne, Australia, has done a brilliant job in summarizing professional consensus about writing text equivalents (Figure 7.1).

A tricky type of graphic that has its own mention in the Success Criterion for Guideline 1.1 is the CAPTCHA, which is used to test that forms are being filled out by people and not software programs that are trying to disseminate spam or worse. Many developers have tried to come up with accessible CAPTCHAs, but these often complicate the issue—a CAPTCHA that requires users to solve a math problem, for example, may be accessible to screen reader users but problematic for some people with cognitive disabilities. Jared Smith, the associate director of the influential accessibility initiative WebAIM (http://webaim.org), has proposed what many see as the best solution: permitting all input and then automatically filtering out the likely spam. His detailed directions are at http://webaim.org/blog/spam_free_accessible_forms.

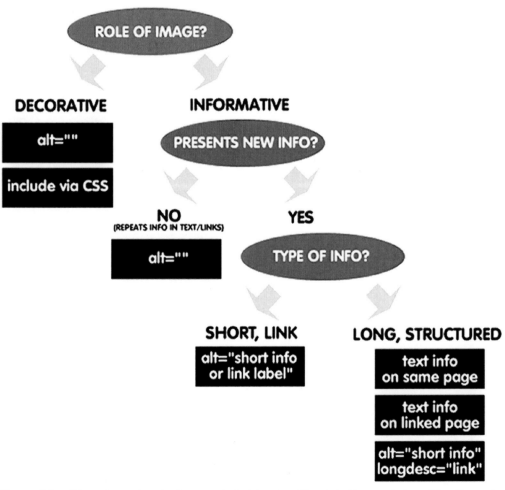

**Figure 7.1.** "Text alternatives for images: A decision tree." *Reprinted by permission of Dey Alexander*

Keep in mind that blind users are not the only individuals who may benefit from text equivalents. For example, people who have low bandwidth may turn off automatic graphics loading; when this happens, the text equivalents become visible, and users can decide whether it will be worthwhile to click on individual images and wait for them to load.

To be fully accessible, multimedia needs to provide alternatives to information presented in either audio- or visual-only forms. The Success Criteria of *Guideline 1.2* cover the strategies for doing this, primarily through captions, audio description, and transcripts. The Level AAA Criterion 1.2.6 also mentions providing sign language interpretation for prerecorded video.

*Guideline 1.3* deals with programmatic determination, which means that users reviewing a page can perceive all information regardless of what assistive technology, browser, or other user agent is active. Programmatic determination is often accomplished through redundancy—for example, a required form field might be marked using visual indicators such as colored or boldface type, which would be hard for screen readers to convey. Adding an asterisk or the text "Required Field" would make it accessible. Markup is also key; for example, using HTML to associate form fields with text labels makes it easy to know the purpose of each field.

The "How to Meet" page for Success Criteria 1.3.1 provides a long list of strategies for accomplishing programmatic determination. Criteria 1.3.2 emphasizes the need for users to be able to determine the correct order in which content is presented where relevant; an example of this is setting up two columns so that screen readers read down one before starting the other, instead of reading across the web page. Criteria 1.3.3 covers providing instructions in a way that does not require sight or hearing—for example, "Select the green button labeled Go" (assuming that the "Go" button has been labeled in a way that a screen reader can access it) instead of simply "Select the green button."

*Guideline 1.4* covers a variety of specific issues that can affect users' ability to effectively perceive information, including use of color (Success Criteria 1.4.1, 1.4.3, and 1.4.6), controlling embedded audio (Success Criteria 1.4.2 and 1.4.7), text presentation (Success Criteria 1.4.4 and 1.4.8), and bitmapped text (text that cannot be selected using the cursor) (Success Criteria 1.4.5 and 1.4.9, which supplement 1.1.1).

## Operable: Guidelines 2.1–2.4

A major advantage of the Internet over print materials is the many opportunities for interaction: links that lead to related information, buttons that submit form information, controls that operate playback of videos. However, if assistive technology users and other individuals with disabilities cannot access these interactive items on a given site, these advantages are irrelevant. The Operable guidelines ensure that people who do not use the computer in standard ways can still operate interactive items.

*Guideline 2.1* explicitly states that all functionality should be operable via keyboard commands—that is, mouse use should not be required. Success Criteria 2.1.1 covers the need of users to be able to get to and operate any interactive item; Criteria 2.1.2 covers avoidance of "keyboard traps" where users can navigate to an interactive object but not away from it.

Interactive items that change too quickly for people with many types of disabilities to access and interact with them can also cause problems. *Guideline 2.2* and its Success Criteria discuss ways that dynamic elements and timeouts can be made accessible.

Some animated items that flash within a particular frequency range (roughly three to fifty times per second) can trigger seizures for people with photosensitive epilepsy. *Guideline 2.3* and its Success Criteria specify ways to avoid using images in this range.

*Guideline 2.4* has a variety of criteria designed to help users effectively navigate among pages and identify the one that they are currently accessing.

## Understandable: Guidelines 3.1–3.3

While it could be argued that both the Perceivable and Operable guidelines contribute to making pages reasonably easy to understand, the three guidelines classified under the Understandable category are directly related to page content. This category has the greatest overlap with overall usability; most of the success criteria here are universally beneficial.

The Level A and AA Success Criteria for *Guideline 3.1* cover identification of the primary language that the page is written in (3.1.1) and any words or phrases that are in a different language (3.1.2). This helps screen readers that support multiple languages know which one to use. The four Level AAA criteria have more to do with intelligibility, encouraging web designers to provide assistance with understanding unusual words (3.1.3), abbreviations (3.1.2), and pronunciation (3.1.4) and to provide assistance with, or alternatives to, text whose readability is above the "lower secondary education level" (3.1.3).

*Guideline 3.2* covers predictability in two areas. The first is for changes of context— for example, pop-up windows and pages that refresh unexpectedly, which can occur with some frequency during regular web browsing. This can be disorienting at the least, particularly to screen reader users. Success Criteria 3.2.1, 3.2.2, and 3.2.5 discourage changes of context unless the user has been warned or given an opportunity to control when the change occurs. The other two criteria are about consistency—how navigation elements such as breadcrumb trails appear on pages within a site (3.2.3) and how elements are labeled (3.2.4).

*Guideline 3.3* deals with error-handling assistance, which was not a part of WCAG 1.0. This includes Success Criteria for avoiding errors (3.3.2, 3.3.5) and efficiently correcting them when they occur (3.3.1, 3.3.3, 3.3.4).

To address this guideline, HTML5 has a "required" attribute for form fields that automatically flag blank required fields in a way that can be accessed by screen readers. More information is available at http://www.wufoo.com/html5/attributes/09-required.html.

## Robust: Guideline 4.1

The single guideline under the "Robust" category does not address specific access needs. Instead, it seeks to ensure compatibility with user agents, including assistive technologies. Think of compliance with this category as being like the high school English teacher who never let you get away with sloppy writing practices. The teacher caused you some extra work, but in the end you were able to write prose that other people found intelligible. Similarly, user agents assume that web page authoring will follow the rules associated with the !DOCTYPE statement on the first line of the page's code (Success Criterion 4.1.1) and that the accessibility standards associated with programming languages such as JavaScript are followed (Success Criterion 4.1.2). Otherwise, pages may not display correctly in browsers, and assistive technologies may convey gibberish to their users.

## Design

> Keeping the design as simple as possible is a good starting point for building a barrier-free Web site. This does not mean there has to be a bland, boring presentation of content. It means that all elements must be chosen deliberately to enhance the content rather than be window dressing or distract from the presentation. (Casey 1999)

The de facto standard for providing an accessible website is to comply with all Level A and AA criteria. When you begin to look at improving the accessibility of your website, a good strategy is to start with the goal of complying with the Level A criteria and then moving on to Level AA. WCAG 2.0 documentation notes, "It is not recommended that Level AAA conformance be required as a general policy for entire sites because it is not possible to satisfy all Level AAA Success Criteria for some content" (Caldwell et al. 2008). However, Level AAA criteria often cover design features that dovetail with general usability principles, such as creating site navigation strategies, helping users prevent errors, and writing using clear language. Even if you decide to conform to Level A or AA, you may still want to ensure compliance with some Level AAA criteria.

The easiest way to promote accessibility is to build it into your web design or redesign process. A good starting place is to examine the proposed functionality of the page. For example, consider whether using carousels (displays of information that changes constantly), videos, or other dynamic items is the right way to communicate the information you want to get across. If it is, tag these as requiring accessibility review. If they are simply used to be "eye-catching," then you may need to weigh the ease of providing accessibility against their general value.

As you develop a design strategy for your site, run it past your accessibility resource people (see chapter 1). Even when you do not yet have anything on the web, showing or describing sketches of proposed pages can net you valuable input about what may or may not work for members of your target audience.

## Coding

To communicate effectively with your webmaster, it may help to know that the coding for almost all web pages has four components.

The first line on the page should be a <!DOCTYPE> declaration indicating the HTML standards to which the page complies. Pages that have a missing or invalid declaration are out of compliance with WCAG (Success Criterion 4.1.1). A list of valid <!DOCTYPE> declarations is at http://www.w3.org/QA/2002/04/valid-dtd-list.html.

> You may have someone in your organization who is insistent on carousel use even in the face of arguments based on accessibility and other considerations. Show them http://shouldiuseacarousel.com.

The second line should be an <HTML> tag, which allows information relevant to the site at large to be specified. For WCAG compliance, the <HTML> tag should include information about the primary language that the website uses (Success Criterion 3.1.1). Information about correctly implementing this language attribute is at http://www.w3.org/TR/WCAG20-TECHS/H57.html. Most sites based in the United States will probably use "en" as the language code, but a list of other codes is at http://www.w3schools.com/tags/ref_language_codes.asp.

The <HTML> tag is followed by a <HEAD> section, which contains background information relevant to the entire document. The page title (Success Criterion 2.4.2) and an external cascading style sheet (multiple success criteria; see http://www.w3.org/TR/WCAG20-TECHS/css.html) are part of the <HEAD> section.

The page title should be added using a <TITLE> tag—for example, <TITLE>Zingerman's Deli Menu</TITLE>. The text should be concise, unique, and descriptive, and it should match at least part of the <h1> heading tag. Keep in mind that this page title is usually the first thing that screen reader users will hear, and, if implemented correctly, it is a powerful navigation aid. If your site is large, it can be helpful to include a vertical bar and the overall name of the site—for example, <TITLE>Accessibility Services | Sunnydale Public Library</TITLE>.

Cascading style sheets control the "look and feel" of the page. External style sheets are preferred since they can be attached to any number of pages, and any design changes—for example font size and color definitions—will have a universal effect, rather than requiring pages to be modified one at a time. An excellent tutorial on external style sheets is at http://webaim.org/techniques/css.

Finally, the <BODY> section contains everything that users will actually perceive and operate, along with more specific background information. Most guidelines are implemented within this section.

Start by looking at the elements you plan to include within the <BODY>. What needs to be perceivable, operable, and understandable for assistive technology users to successfully access your site? The following is a list of several common elements along with resources for making them WCAG compliant:

*Text equivalents:* http://webaim.org/techniques/alttext

*Form fields:* http://webaim.org/techniques/forms/controls

*Tables:* http://webaim.org/techniques/tables

*Captioning and audio description for multimedia:* http://ncam.wgbh.org/invent_build/web_multimedia/tools-guidelines

*Headings:* http://webaim.org/techniques/semanticstructure

*Skip-navigation links:* http://webaim.org/techniques/skipnav

*Avoiding keyboard traps:* http://www.nomensa.com/blog/2011/keyboard-traps

As much as possible, create HTML templates that include correct markup. That way, if multiple people are working on your site, they will not need to repeatedly re-create your work.

# @ Evaluating for Accessibility

A common step in any website implementation is to review the site by testing it for technical issues (Does it look alright when viewed in common browsers? Does the Search function bring up logical results?) and usability (Can patrons use the site to find library hours? Do they like the overall layout?). Including an accessibility review in this process will ensure that problems are identified and addressed before the site is made public.

If the website is large, it is not necessary to check every page. A rule of thumb is to check about 10 to 15 percent of pages, being sure to include any page that has features unique or unusual within the site such as forms, tables, and multimedia.

## Automated Testing Tools

A variety of tools are available to help with testing websites for compliance with WCAG and/or other guidelines. W3C maintains a list of tools at http://www.w3.org/WAI/RC/tools/complete.

Be aware that even the best checker cannot fully assess compliance with the spirit rather than the letter of accessibility guidelines. For example, general checkers may tell you if a graphic has a text equivalent but not if the equivalent content is appropriate. Other guidelines require direct inspection, such as Success Criterion 1.3.3: "Instructions provided for understanding and operating content do not rely solely on sensory characteristics of components such as shape, size, visual location, orientation, or sound" (W3C 2013). Automated checkers are not going to be able to parse the meaning of instructions to determine whether this guideline is being followed; a human will need to perform a review.

Many of the best tools are free and readily available online. These include the following.

### General Checkers

These tools can be used to check compliance with multiple guidelines.

The *WAVE toolbar* from WebAIM is a good go-to tool, particularly for quick assessments. At present, it is available in two formats: as a Firefox plug-in that can be downloaded from http://wave.webaim.org/toolbar and appears in the browser window as a toolbar at the top of the page when installed or as an online version at http://five.wave. webaim.org. Some pages may work better with one format or the other, so it is useful to know about both.

Both versions of WAVE tag problems with icons via one of three colors: green icons to indicate compliance ("features"), yellow for potential problems ("alerts"), and red to indicate accessibility violations ("errors"). Clicking on the "Icons Key" on the WAVE toolbar brings up a new view that describe each icon. After some experience using WAVE, you will likely find yourself remembering the meaning of the icons that appear most often.

The WAVE plug-in can be downloaded from http://wave.webaim.org/toolbar. WAVE can also be run directly from this site, but this version will not work with pages that are behind a firewall or are otherwise not generally available. When WAVE results are not clear or conclusive, the Web Accessibility Toolbar for Internet Explorer can be used to obtain more information. Unlike WAVE, which does a general page check, the Web Accessibility Initiative toolbar can be used to check for specific items one at a time.

If you are using the WAVE plug-in on a page that generates many messages, the icons may get squished together and it is hard to see where all the errors and alerts are or what they apply to. If this happens, click the "Disable Styles" option on the toolbar. The page will create a linearized version that will let you see all the icons in context.

The toolbar can be downloaded from http://tinyurl.com/b9dmhbo. Basic documentation for using the toolbar is available from http://tinyurl.com/bylwzj5.

*AChecker* is a tool for generating technical reports that can be turned over to programmers for addressing many types of issues, especially if your programmers have enough experience with accessibility to assign useful text equivalents and otherwise extrapolate solutions. The report includes three tabs: Known Problems (clear accessibility violations caused by missing code, insufficient color contrast, etc.), Likely Problems (e.g., text equivalents that may be too long or inaccurate), and Potential Problems (e.g., heading markup that might be being used incorrectly). AChecker can be run online from http://achecker.ca.

AChecker does tend to go overboard in pointing out Potential Problems. It is usually alright to ignore this set of results; anything that is a genuine issue should show up in one of the other tests or in the functional testing (see p. 108).

The *Functional Accessibility Evaluator* was developed by the University of Illinois, and it provides results similar to WAVE in a more report-like format. Useful features include statistical reports on compliance and a sophisticated ability to analyze changing content. Individual pages can be analyzed by going to http://fae.cita.uiuc.edu; signing up with the Functional Accessibility Evaluator (free) allows multiple pages to be analyzed at a time.

## Specialty Checkers

These tools are primarily relevant to a single WCAG guideline.

*W3C Markup Validation Service* (http://validator.w3.org) checks pages for valid code (Success Criterion 4.1.1). Like AChecker, it provides error reports that can be given directly to programmers; wherever possible, it also suggests fixes. Reports will often contain multiple error messages that can be addressed by making a single fix. Because the report is easy and fast to generate, try rerunning it multiple times to check fixes as you implement them.

The *Colour Contrast Analyser* can be downloaded from http://www.paciellogroup.com/resources/contrastAnalyser. It provides a good balance between thoroughness and ease of use for assessing the contrast ratio between text and background colors, and it will tell you if Success Criteria 1.4.3 (Level AA) and 1.4.6 (Level AAA) are met for text at standard and large sizes (large is defined as more than 18-point regular text or more than 14-point boldface text). It is easy to use for spot-checking—an eyedropper icon is used to "pick up" the background and foreground colors for comparison. In addition to the results, the picked-up colors are displayed as samples; if the contrast fails to meet the success criteria, an arrow to the right of the color sample can be clicked to reveal multiple options for making the color contrast compliant.

Black text on a white background provides the highest level of contrast but is not automatically the best choice, particularly since people with learning disabilities may be distracted by excessive white space or glare. Cream or light gray backgrounds reduce these issues while still providing high contrast.

## Readability Testing

WCAG Guideline 3.1 ("Make text content readable and understandable") is one of the widely applicable criteria in WCAG; people with cognitive disabilities benefit from readable text, but so do individuals whose first language is not English, individuals with limited schooling, and pretty much everyone else. One common and easy-to-understand measure of readability is the *Flesch Reading Ease* score, which ranges from 100 (a likely score for baby's board books) to 0 (the most tenebrous and amphibological writing possible). A good score for most prose is 60. The Flesch score is based on the average number of syllables per word and words per sentence; using words with fewer syllables and shorter sentences is likely to raise your score.

The *Juicy Studio Readability Test* (juicystudio.com/services/readability.php) calculates the Flesch score and performs other readability tests for one page at a time. It also provides data on word and sentence length for the page being analyzed.

As noted earlier, content flashing within a certain speed range may trigger seizures in people with photosensitive epilepsy (Success Criterion 2.3.1, Level A, and 2.3.2, Level AAA). Where flashing content is essential to use of the site, the Photosensitive Epilepsy Analysis Tool (http://trace.wisc.edu/peat) can be used to check whether it passes these criteria.

## Functional Testing

Compliance with one or more of the sets of web accessibility guidelines is an important first step. However, to ensure accessibility, it is also necessary to test how the pages actually work with assistive technologies—at a minimum, with those technologies available at the library and, ideally, with any additional technologies that patrons most frequently report using to access library web pages from other locations. This is called *functional testing*.

To understand why functional testing is important, think about times that you have used a map to plan out a driving route, only to find that when you are actually on the road, there is construction, accidents, and other barriers that a map does not predict. Similarly, web pages can pass all guideline tests and still have accessibility or usability problems.

Ideally, all functional testing should be done by individuals who use assistive technology to meet their own needs on a regular basis. However, in most cases, it is possible for a library staff member who has a working knowledge of a piece of assistive technology to perform the testing. Screen readers are an exception; it is simply not possible for a sighted person to experience screen reader use in the same way as a blind individual.

To ensure the efficiency of functional testing, it helps to create a test plan to guide testers. This plan does not need to be long, but it should include the primary site features that people will need to access. When creating the plan, try to describe tasks or ask questions ("Find the hours that the library is open," "What is the name of the library director?") rather than list procedures ("Go to the About page, navigate to the bottom, and find the Accessibility link"). A sample test plan is provided in appendix C.

Encourage testers to provide information about how they completed the task. If a user says, "It took me five minutes to find the library hours" or "I had to go to three different pages to find when you were open," it can serve as a heads-up that not only might people with disabilities have difficulty completing the task but nondisabled patrons or patrons who do not use assistive technology might also find site usability to be less than ideal.

Recruit testers from your community, starting with your accessibility resource people. Because thorough testing can take a good chunk of time, find a way to provide some type of recompense—check with your testers to see if they would prefer money, gift cards, and so forth.

## Documentation

Once you have built accessibility into your site, you will want to let people know about it. It is helpful both to trumpet the fact that you have paid attention to accessibility (so that visitors know to expect a positive experience) and to provide details on any features, such as keyboard shortcuts (key presses that emulate mouse functionality) or conforming alternative versions. The Library of Congress has a good basic page of such documentation at http://www.loc.gov/access/web.html.

Sometimes assistive technologies will not work with a page as expected, but a work-around can be discovered during the testing process by a sophisticated user. For example, a speech input user may find that she or he cannot activate a particular link by saying its name, but there is a logical, mnemonic keyboard shortcut that can be spoken instead. There may also be known problems with specific browsers and/or assistive technologies—such as the inability of Internet Explorer 5, 6, and 7 to work with skip-navs or any other same-page links. Provide documentation on your website to let people know about these work-arounds and known problems.

Make sure that links to your accessibility-related documentation are located in a prominent place. An early link on the home page is a good start. You should also provide multiple contact methods for the webmaster or other responsible person in case people have questions or find a problem.

## Getting Started With Web Accessibility

### In-House Development

Understandably, the first question that many website developers ask when approached about accessibility is "What are some good models?" This has proven an unexpectedly hard question to answer, largely because of the mutable nature of web pages. For example, a page that was going to be cited here as an example of a creative solution to a tricky issue had been completely changed by the time that the book was ready for publication.

No one has created a repository of accessible web page designs. However, there are a couple of strategies to try when looking for examples of solutions to particular design issues.

First, the WCAG 2.0 (http://www.w3.org/TR/UNDERSTANDING-WCAG20/intro.html) and WebAIM (http://webaim.org) sites contain many examples of accessible code. They also tend to walk the walk by ensuring that their own sites are accessible. If you find an element of interest that is an actual part of one of these websites, such as a form or table, try using the automated checkers to ensure that it is compliant and then pass it along to your developer as a good model.

Next, do an online search for "accessible" plus the name of the element you want to know about. For example, carousels are a common website element used to display pictures and information; these often move far too fast for assistive technology users and people who have reading difficulties to interpret. Doing a search for "accessible carousels" will bring up Sarah Pulis's explanation of how to allow users to control carousels so that they can access their information (http://www.accessiq.org/create/content/anatomy-of-an-accessible-carousel). Your search may also turn up information about how to use alternatives to the given element. The first result in the "accessible carousels" search brings up an interview with Jared Smith where he argues against any carousel use, instead advocating for "better content and design decisions—what is the most important content and how can I present it in a meaningful, simple, and accessible way?" (Netmag 2013).

## Prioritization

If you are considering web accessibility for the first time and already have a website, it can be difficult to know where to start. In practice, retrofitting a website has much in common with retrofitting a building: in both cases, it is better to start doing small things and build up to the more elaborate issues rather than becoming daunted.

The University of Michigan has a site at http://hr.umich.edu/webaccess that provides great overview of web accessibility basics. In particular, the "Best Practices" area (http://hr.umich.edu/webaccess/best) provides straightforward guidance on "low-hanging fruit"—issues that can cause significant problems but are relatively easy to fix. These include adding text equivalents to graphics and using small pieces of code to make tables and forms accessible.

## Raising Awareness

You may encounter resistance from administrators or others who feel that implementing web accessibility is "too much work" or that "no one will sue us." One strategy for addressing this is empathy: if you can show people what it can be like to use assistive technology and just how hard it could be to interface with inaccessible websites, they may agree to at least begin addressing accessibility issues. As WebAIM's accessibility director Jared Smith has said, "we've found demonstrating accessibility issues—such as listening to a page in a screen reader—is the best way to make people acutely aware of the end user impact" (Netmag 2013).

WebAIM has two terrific simulations of using screen readers (see chapter 6) and magnification software. Explanations and links to the simulations are at http://webaim.org/simulations/screenreader/ and http://webaim.org/simulations/lowvision, respectively.

One way to simulate the experience of having a learning disability is to show people the following printed text and ask them to interpret it:

Ανδ σο εῶεν τηουγη ωε φαχε τηε διφφιχυλτιεσ οφ τοδαψ ανδ τομορρω, I στιλλ ηαῶε α δρεαμ. Ιτ ισ α δρεαμ δεεπλψ ροοτεδ ιν τηε Αμεριχαν δρεαμ.Iηαῶε α δρεαμ τηατ ονε δαψ τηισ νατιον ωιλλ ρισε υπ ανδ λιῶε ουτ τηε τρυε μεανινγ οφ ιτσ χρεεδ: "Ωε ηολδ τηεσε τρυτησ το βε σελφ–εῶιδεντ, τηατ αλλ μεν αρε χρεατεδ εθυαλ." I ηαῶε α δρεαμ τηατ ονε δαψ ον τηε ρεδ ηιλλσ οφ Γεοργια, τηε σονσ οφ φορμερ σλαῶεσ ανδ τηε σονσ οφ φορμερ σλαῶε οωνερσ ωιλλ βε αβλε το σιτ δοων τογετηερ ατ τηε ταβλε οφ βροτηερηοοδ. I ηαῶε α δρεαμ τηατ ονε δαψ εῶεν τηε στατε οφ. Μισσισσιππι, α στατε σωελτερινγ ωιτη τηε ηεατ οφ ινφυστιχε, σωελτερινγ ωιτη τηε ηεατ οφ οππρεσσιον, ωιλλ βε τρανσφορμεδ ιντο αν οασισ οφ φρεεδομ ανδ φυστιχε. I ηαῶε α δρεαμ τηατ μψ φουρ λιττλε χηιλδρεν ωιλλ ονε δαψ λιῶε ιν α νατιον ωηερε τηεψ ωιλλ νοτ βε φυδγεδ βψ τηε χολορ οφ τηειρ σκιν βυτ βψ τηε χοντεντ οφ τηειρ χηαραχτερ. I ηαῶε α δρεαμ τοδαψ.

Then ask them to listen while you read the original text (available at http://tinyurl. com/kkjlzr7) aloud and see if the multimedia presentation makes it easier to decode, especially for a phrase that is repeated throughout the excerpt.

## Authoring Software

Many libraries and other organizations now use content management systems such as WordPress, Drupal, Plone, and Joomla, or simple authoring programs, such as Google Sites, to create web pages. Be aware that these programs often do not allow coding access to anything other than the <BODY> section and therefore may not permit full compliance with guidelines. Content management systems usually discuss accessibility somewhere in their documentation.

*WordPress:* The main Accessibility page is at http://codex.wordpress.org/Accessibility. There is also a blog for the WordPress accessibility group at http://make.wordpress. org/accessibility.

*Drupal:* Two useful sites are Accessibility Tools and Best Practices for Site Builders (http://drupal.org/node/394094) and Creating Accessible Themes (http://drupal. org/node/464472).

*Joomla:* Joomla has an accessibility statement at http://www.joomla.org/accessibility-statement.html. Some accessibility extensions for use with Joomla are at http:// extensions.joomla.org/extensions/style-a-design/accessibility.

*Plone:* An article on Improving Accessibility for your Plone sites is at http://plone.org/ documentation/kb/improving-accessibility-for-your-plone-sites/tutorial-all-pages.

Most content management systems use themes to facilitate designing the look and feel of a site, and you may want to do some research on whether someone has created a theme with accessibility in mind. Searching theme lists and discussion forums may prove fruitful.

Google Sites allows many guidelines to be implemented. Exceptions and work-arounds are discussed at http://tinyurl.com/aa8qqob.

## Alternate Versions

The Conformance Requirements for WCAG 2.0 specifically mention providing a "conforming alternative version" if the standard page cannot be made to meet the desired conformance level. In the past, this was seen as a strategy of last resort by many web accessibility experts; one of the counterarguments was the concern that an alternative version would not have the same functionality or maintenance schedule as the standard version.

The proliferation of mobile devices and the subsequent development of alternative, mobile-friendly websites has in many ways been a breakthrough for helping developers understand and implement accessibility. On June 29, 2007, about one hundred thousand mostly young, mostly affluent Americans suddenly ran into accessibility barriers. That is the date that people started buying iPhones. Those iPhones did not support Flash—a programming technology used to create multimedia, games, and other sophisticated applications—and for reasons at least as much political as technical, neither do iPhones in 2013. Flash is also notoriously incompatible with screen readers. So if you are blind, an iPhone user, or both, you will not perceive anything in Flash.

It would have been difficult even five years ago to predict the frequency with which people now access web pages using devices with small displays, no mice, virtual keyboards, and restricted access to some types of scripted objects. Developers who create pages that either transform when a mobile device is detected or provide a mobile-specific version have the opportunity to plan for compatibility with a range of devices, regardless of whether they are used for accessibility or convenience (or both). As Debra Riley-Huff (2012, 34) writes, "everything about designing for mobile [devices] works for accessibility, and this includes minimalism, touch accuracy, speed, HTML5, semantic markup, and graceful fallback solutions. Having your website be mobile-first or mobile-ready is an excellent goal and will greatly increase its accessibility."

Keep in mind that to meet accessibility requirements, any conforming alternative version, including the mobile site, must have equivalent functionality to the standard version. For example, if you have a mobile or other alternative version of an online catalog that leaves out features from the standard version, such as placing holds on items, this version cannot be considered accessible.

## Limitations of Guidelines

As powerful as web accessibility guidelines can be, they cannot predict all barriers, nor can they predict individual user behavior, prior experience, and preferences. Three examples of guideline limitations are access keys, text equivalents for decorative photographs, and default print size.

### Access Keys

WCAG 1.0 (1999) contained a guideline on providing keyboard shortcuts to "important links (including those in client-side image maps), form controls, and groups of form controls." Even though this was a Priority 3 guideline, it caught the attention of many web developers who were happy to include "access keys" in their pages. Unfortunately, there can be two problems with this. One was that developers did not always include documentation for their access keys, so no one knew they were there. A more critical issue is that some access keys were identical to keyboard commands that are a part of assistive technologies, so users might find that their screen reader or other assistive software would not work properly on a given site. Access keys are no longer required in any part of WCAG 2.0, although they can be used to meet Success Criterion 2.4.1. The accessibility resource WebAIM (2013b) periodically conducts surveys of the preferences of screen reader users; between its January 2009 and December 2010 surveys (see WebAIM 2013a, 2013b, 2013c), the number of individuals who reported frequent use of access keys dropped from 38 to 27.5 percent, further indicating that access keys are not as useful as they might appear.

## Text Equivalents for Decorative Photographs

The January 2009 WebAIM (2013b) survey also included a question about whether and how decorative photos should be identified using a text equivalent. Respondents who self-identified as not having a disability tended to say that it should not be identified in the text equivalent, while actual screen reader users preferred at least a basic description, such as "Photo of smiling lady." The survey analysis notes, "We cannot help but think that blind screen reader users might find their experiences less enjoyable if *all* such images, which are typically unidentified now, were suddenly identified to them. This underscores WebAIM's long held notion that providing proper, equivalent alternative text is the most difficult aspect of web accessibility."

## Default Print Size

WCAG 2.0 does not contain any success criteria about default font sizes; it only specifies that text can be enlarged up to 200 percent without using assistive technology, for example, by changing browser settings (Success Criterion 1.4.4). It is perfectly possible therefore to have very small type on a page and still have it pass WCAG 2.0. However, since use of small print negatively affects many individuals who may not even think about modifying font size—millions of aging baby boomers, for a start—it cannot be considered a good practice.

# External Vendors

If you are considering acquisition of any web-based product, accessibility should be included during your evaluation process along with price, compatibility, and other natural considerations. A relevant tool that is part of Section 508 implementation is the Voluntary Product Accessibility Template (VPAT). This is a document intended to allow communication about compliance of websites and other items covered by Section 508. Each 508 criterion is usually given one of four ratings: Supports, Supports with Exceptions, Does Not Support, or Not Applicable.

As the tool's name implies, vendors are not obligated to create VPATs for their products. There is also no requirement that someone outside the company or someone with accessibility knowledge fill out the form, so there is no guarantee of either objectivity or accuracy. Nonetheless, as part of your procurement process, it is good practice to ask vendors if they have a VPAT; at a minimum, this can give you a feel for their awareness and commitment to accessibility. If they do not already have a VPAT but request guidance on creating one, Even Grounds Consulting has a useful basic guide available at http://www .evengrounds.com/articles/creating-an-effective-vpat.

When you receive a VPAT, review it carefully. It is often encouraging to see at least one "Supports with Exceptions" or "Does Not Support" ranking, since this indicates that the form has been filled out after some actual testing rather than simply submitted with pro forma indications of support. Ask the vendor for details about any unexplained rankings indicating noncompliance, including their plans and timeline for providing fixes.

Although the VPAT is supposed to be a public document, an increasing number of companies are indicating that they have a VPAT but are unwilling to share it. Encourage them to talk with their lawyers and reconsider this stance.

At this time, there is no official equivalent of the VPAT for WCAG 2.0. However, the Minnesota Department of Health has created a form that can be used for reporting compliance with all three WCAG levels. The PDF of the form is available at http://www.health.state.mn.us/divs/fh/mch/fhv/documents/mi_vpat_wcag2_standards.pdf.

There are still some vendors that claim compliance with WCAG 1.0. Because this is a significantly outdated standard, it should not be relied on as evidence of accessibility.

## Web Accessibility Decision Points

*What web accessibility guidelines will your library follow? If you choose to use WCAG 2.0, what level of compliance will you aim for?* Most library websites are fairly straightforward. There might be a few videos to caption and some form fields associated with searching the catalog that need to be labeled, but otherwise the complexity level is fairly low. In these instances, full Level AA compliance with WCAG should be possible. However, there may be clear reasons for you to choose a different compliance level or set of guidelines. For example, if you are planning a major redesign of your website in the near future, you might make changes now to bring your site into compliance with Section 508 and then build WCAG Level AA compliance into the redesign.

*Who will take responsibility for ensuring web page accessibility?* It can be exceptionally frustrating to depend on a website for an accessible experience, only to have that experience disappear when the site is updated or replaced. Even worse is the situation of calling the site provider and being told, "Oh, the person responsible for the accessibility of our website has left." Responsibility may lie directly with the webmaster or with another member of the library staff. However, it should be an ongoing part of at least one job description, and information about the library's accessibility policies and practices should be kept in a form that will be easy to pass along.

*How will the site's accessibility be promoted and tracked?* Many libraries have an Accessibility page explaining the library's commitment to accessibility, highlighting specific features, and providing the name of a contact for questions or comments. Cortland (IL) Community Library has a good model at http://www.cortlandlibrary.com/Website%20Accessibility%20Policy.html. Remember to provide a prominent link to this page from your home page and other relevant pages throughout the site.

Even the most thorough accessibility review may miss some issues. You will also want to make sure that the Accessibility page and, ideally, one or more other prominent spots within the site have clear instructions on how people can report accessibility errors that they encounter.

# ⑥ Key Points

Web accessibility is often seen as daunting, but with understanding and regular attention, it can become simply another consideration that the library uses in creating and maintaining its websites. Keeping a paper trail of what you have done to implement accessibility will be important in making sure that the library's accessibility standards are maintained regardless of staff turnover. Maintaining communication with site users will ensure that any problems are identified so that they can be addressed in a timely and ongoing manner.

The topics that have been covered so far in this book address common accessibility needs that libraries might encounter. However, there is always the possibility that patrons may have unanticipated requests or run into unexpected barriers. Chapter 8 covers these, as well as thoughts for how to incorporate accessibility more organically into the library field.

# ⑥ References

American Library Association. 2009. "Resolution on Accessibility for Library Websites." http://tinyurl.com/kf3roml.

Caldwell, Ben, et al. 2008. "Web Content Accessibility Guidelines (WCAG) 2.0." http://www.w3.org/TR/WCAG20/.

Casey, Carol. 1999. "Accessibility in the Virtual Library: Creating Equal Opportunity Web Sites." *Information Technology and Libraries* 18, no. 1: 22–25.

European Commission. 2012. *Proposal for a Directive of the European Parliament and of the Council on the Accessibility of Public Sector Bodies' Websites.* http://ec.europa.eu/information_society/newsroom/cf//document.cfm?doc_id=1242.

Fulton, Camilla. 2011. "Web Accessibility, Libraries, and the Law." *Information Technology and Libraries* 30, no. 1: 34–43.

Netmag (blog). 2013. "Accessibility Expert Warns: Stop Using Carousels." July 10. http://www.creativebloq.com/accessibility-expert-warns-stop-using-carousels-7133778.

Riley-Huff, Debra. 2012. "Web Accessibility and Universal Design: A Primer on Standards and Best Practices for Libraries." *Library Technology Reports* 48, no. 7: 34.

Vu, Minh N. 2013. "Justice Department Pushes Back Date for Proposed Website Accessibility Rules—Yet Again." ADA Title III (blog). July 29. http://www.adatitleiii.com/2013/07/justice-department-pushes-back-date-for-proposed-website-accessibility-rules-yet-again/.

WebAIM. 2013a. "Screen Reader User Survey #2 Results." http://webaim.org/projects/screenreadersurvey2/.

———. 2013b. "Screen Reader User Survey #3 Results." http://webaim.org/projects/screenreadersurvey3.

———. 2013c. "Survey of Preferences of Screen Readers Users," http://webaim.org/projects/screenreadersurvey.

Wikipedia. 2013. "Five Laws of Library Science." Wikipedia. February 28. http://en.wikipedia.org/wiki/Five_laws_of_library_science.

World Wide Web Consortium (W3C). 2008. "Web Content Accessibility Guidelines (WCAG) 2.0." http://www.w3.org/TR/WCAG20/.

———. 2011. "Definition of User Agent." WAI UA Wiki. http://www.w3.org/WAI/UA/work/wiki/Definition_of_User_Agent.

———. 2012. "W3C Web Content Accessibility Guidelines 2.0 Approved as ISO/IEC International Standard." http://www.w3.org/2012/07/wcag2pas-pr.html.

———. 2013. "Sensory Characteristics." http://www.w3.org/TR/UNDERSTANDING-WCAG 20/content-structure-separation-understanding.html.

# ◎ Resources

## Guidelines and How-To Information

Cady, John, and Jane Vincent. 2013. "Sites and Web Page Accessibility." http://tinyurl.com/aa8qqob.

Drupal.org. 2012. "Creating Accessible Themes." http://drupal.org/node/464472.

———. 2013. "Accessibility Tools and Best Practices for Site Builders." http://drupal.org/node/394094.

Geisler, Zennith. 2013. "Anatomy of an Accessible Carousel." Access IQ (blog). March 26. http://www.accessiq.org/create/content/anatomy-of-an-accessible-carousel.

Hillen, Hans. 2013. "Accessible jQuery-ui Components Demonstration." http://hanshillen.github.io/jqtest/.

Joomla. 2013a. "Accessibility." http://extensions.joomla.org/extensions/style-a-design/accessibility.

———. 2013b. "Accessibility Statement." http://www.joomla.org/accessibility-statement.html.

National Center for Accessible Media. 2009. "Tools & Guidelines." http://ncam.wgbh.org/invent_build/web_multimedia/tools-guidelines.

Nomensa (blog). 2011. "Keyboard Traps." http://www.nomensa.com/blog/2011/keyboard-traps/. April 13.

Plone. 2012. "Improving Accessibility for Your Plone Sites." http://plone.org/documentation/kb/improving-accessibility-for-your-plone-sites/tutorial-all-pages.

Smith, Jared. 2007. "Spam-Free Accessible Forms." WebAIM (blog). March 7. http://webaim.org/blog/spam_free_accessible_forms/.

W3C Quality Assurance. 2011. "Recommended Doctype Declarations to Use in Your Web Document." http://www.w3.org/QA/2002/04/valid-dtd-list.html.

W3CSchools.com. 2013. "HTML Language Code Reference." http://www.w3schools.com/tags/ref_language_codes.asp.

Web Accessibility Initiative. 2009. "Comparison of WCAG 1.0 Checkpoints to WCAG 2.0, in Numerical Order." http://www.w3.org/WAI/WCAG20/from10/comparison/.

WebAIM. 2013a. "Alternative Text." http://webaim.org/techniques/alttext/.

———. 2013b. "Creating Accessible CSS." http://webaim.org/techniques/css/.

———. 2013c. "Creating Accessible Forms: Accessible Form Controls." http://webaim.org/techniques/forms/controls.

———. 2013d. "Creating Accessible Tables." http://webaim.org/techniques/tables/.

———. 2013e. "Low Vision Simulation." http://webaim.org/simulations/lowvision.

———. 2013f. "Screen Reader Simulation." http://webaim.org/simulations/screenreader/.

———. 2013g. "Semantic Structure." http://webaim.org/techniques/semanticstructure/.

———. 2013h. "'Skip Navigation' Links." http://webaim.org/techniques/skipnav/.

Williams, Scott. 2011. "Web Accessibility at the U-M." http://hr.umich.edu/webaccess/.

WordPress.org. 2013a. "Accessibility." http://codex.wordpress.org/Accessibility.

WordPress.org. 2013b. Make WordPress Accessible (blog). http://make.wordpress.org/accessibility/.

World Wide Web Consortium. 2013. "Introduction to Understanding WCAG 2.0." http://www.w3.org/TR/UNDERSTANDING-WCAG20/intro.html.

Wufoo. 2013. "The Required Attribute." http://www.wufoo.com/html5/attributes/09-required.html.

## Web Accessibility Evaluation Tools

AChecker. http://achecker.ca.

Contrast Analyser for Windows and Mac. http://www.paciellogroup.com/resources/contrast Analyser.

Functional Accessibility Evaluator 1.1. http://fae.cita.uiuc.edu.

Juicy Studio Readability Test. http://juicystudio.com/services/readability.php.

Photosensitive Epilepsy Analysis Tool. http://trace.wisc.edu/peat/.

W3C Markup Validation Service. http://validator.w3.org.

WAVE Toolbar. http://wave.webaim.org/toolbar/.

WAVE Web Accessibility Evaluation Tool. http://five.wave.webaim.org.

Web Accessibility Initiative. 2012. "Complete List of Web Accessibility Evaluation Tools." http://www.w3.org/WAI/RC/tools/complete.

Web Accessibility Toolbar. http://tinyurl.com/b9dmhbo.

## Miscellaneous

Cortland Community Library. 2011. "Policies and Procedures: Website Accessibility Policy." http://www.cortlandlibrary.com/Website%20Accessibility%20Policy.html.

Dick, Wayne, and Tom Jewett. 2009. "Mapping Section 508 to WCAG 2.0." http://www.tom jewett.com/accessibility/508–WCAG2.html.

Even Grounds. 2013. "Creating An Effective Voluntary Product Accessibility Template (VPAT)." http://www.evengrounds.com/articles/creating-an-effective-vpat.

Library of Congress. 2013. "Web Site Access." http://www.loc.gov/access/web.html.

Minnesota Department of Health. 2013. "VPAT Web Content Accessibility Guidelines 2.0 level AA." http://www.health.state.mn.us/divs/fh/mch/fhv/documents/mi_vpat_wcag2_standards .pdf.

## Other Resources

Association of Specialized and Cooperative Library Agencies. 2013. "Internet and Web-Based Content Accessibility Checklist." http://www.ala.org/ascla/asclaprotools/thinkaccessible/ internetwebguidelines.

ClearHelper. 2013. "Web Accessibility Blogs." http://www.clearhelper.org/Resources/GWA/ Blogs/.

Individuals who have particularly useful Twitter feeds related to web accessibility include @mpaciello, @swimsy, @JrandomF, and @jared_w_smith.

LinkedIn groups that focus on or frequently discuss web accessibility include the Library and Museum Accessibility Forum, the Modern Web Accessibility Forum, Accessible Technology Policy Group, and the Mobile and Tablet Accessibility Forum.

Swan, Henny. 2013. iheni (blog). http://www.iheni.com.

Thatcher, Jim. "Web Accessibility for Section 508." http://jimthatcher.com/webcourse1.htm.

WebAIM has a forum where the top web accessibility experts pose their hardest questions and conduct lively technical conversations. Sign up and access the archives at http://webaim.org/ discussion/.

# The Accessible Library

---

---

Hard to narrow it down to just one thing [that I wish people would "get" about disability] but I'd say it's that we're neither a tragedy or brave—we're just people doing what we've got to do to make a life. (Bonnie Lewkowicz, open-air accessibility specialist and dancer, 2013)

PEOPLE WITH DISABILITIES ARE IDIOSYNCRATIC, BUT SO ARE LIBRARIES— there are few, if any, one-size-fits-all strategies for implementing accommodations. If there is one constant, it is that libraries and user needs both change over time, and it will not be sufficient to implement accessibility once and assume that you are done. True accessibility—like other facets of library infrastructure, such as security and budget—will need to be addressed on an ongoing basis.

The topics covered in this book are not, of course, exhaustive in regard to what patrons may request or what changes in legislation may require. For any issue, there may be resistance from library administration about implementation or disappointment from patrons if their request is turned down. This chapter provides some suggestions about how to handle both these situations.

Finally, it should be kept in mind that accessibility is not ultimately about architecture and technology and sign language interpreters. Like most library functions, it is about providing optimal service to patrons. The best way to ensure such service is through enhanced awareness of this contingent of patrons—in your library and in the library profession. We now look at some ways that this might be accomplished.

Even if you see a clear case for implementing an accommodation, your administration or other parties responsible for the actual implementation may not agree. Instead of simply approaching them with your request on an ad hoc basis, you may find it necessary to create a business case laying out your rationale for why the accommodation is needed. Your business case may involve the following components.

*Precedents.* Through research or communication with other libraries and public entities (e.g., via resources listed at the end of other chapters), try to document situations where the accommodation has been put in place. Was this experience successful? If not, are there lessons to be learned that might improve your emulation of the model?

*Funding.* Is there a cost involved with implementing this accommodation? If it is significant, where can funding be sought? Get input from the librarian who is responsible for seeking grants for your library, the Friends of the Library group, the Board of Directors, the library foundation, and other likely resources.

*Positive impact if implemented.* Will implementing this accommodation make it easier for people to take advantage of the library's services? Will it create a good public relations opportunity for the library? Can it benefit a range of users, not just those covered by the ADA?

*Negative impact if not implemented.* Legal implications may be part of this, but they should not be the only consideration. Will the failure to implement this dissuade many patrons from coming to the library? Will it be significantly more expensive to implement at a future date?

*Internal supportive statements.* Discuss the request with other staff members to see what they might be able to contribute. Is a supervisor able to dedicate a portion of a staff member's time to implement the accommodation? Is a tech support team member willing to research how a new piece of assistive software can work with the existing network?

*External supportive statements.* Check with your accessibility resource people (see chapter 1) to see if they are willing to provide affidavits. If politically appropriate, try soliciting statements from other influential people, such as a library board member or local politician.

The Association of College and Research Libraries has developed a document called "The Power of Personal Persuasion: Advancing the Academic Library Agenda from the Front Lines," which may be useful in this process. This document is available for free from http://www.ala.org/acrl/sites/ala.org.acrl/files/content/issues/marketing/advocacy_toolkit.pdf.

You may also find that some accommodations can be implemented in stages. As a model, Brian Herzog (2012) has a wonderful article about a request from an older patron to use the library's shredder for a huge number of materials. His immediate solution was to suggest that she contact her local bank, but then he began thinking, "This is a perfect service for libraries to offer. A heavy-duty shredder is something not everyone can afford, but something the community could purchase and share (just like other library materials)." The article ends with a series of due diligence questions to see if this vision will make sense to accomplish.

While a librarian's first reaction to an accommodation request should be "Can we make this happen?" not "Is this an undue burden?" patrons may make requests that do fall outside the bounds of reasonable accommodation. While you may decide to implement some of these anyway, others will likely need to be turned down (at least initially) due to budget, time, or other constraints.

First, check with legal counsel and confirm that implementing the request would qualify as an undue burden or would be otherwise outside the library's obligations. Your next task may then involve the tricky business of saying no while still helping to address the need and maintaining the user's positive impression of the library. The following suggestions may help make bad news easier to deliver to any patron, regardless of whether one has a disability.

*Apologize.* A sincere apology for the library's inability to meet the request can go a long way in maintaining lines of communication with any patron, whether or not "fault" is involved. Carl D. Schneider (2006) suggests that three components be involved in an apology:

*Acknowledgment:* Regardless of the nature of the request, taking the effort to make it indicates that it held some level of importance to the patron. Acknowledging this as part of the apology will likely assure the patron that his or her needs have at least been heard.

*Affect:* According to Schneider (2006), genuine regret needs to be part of the apology. If you think that it will be difficult to communicate this in person, try sending a letter or an e-mail, following any library policies about written communications.

*Vulnerability:* The apology should be nondefensive and should implicitly acknowledge that the patron may not be mollified. However, as the classic book on negotiation *Getting to Yes* points out, "on many occasions an apology can defuse emotions effectively" (Fisher and Ury 1981, 33).

*Continue the reference interview.* Is it important to the patron that she or he be able to use the requested equipment or receive the requested service at the library and nowhere else? If not, check with your accessibility resource people to see where else the patron might be able to locally access the equipment or service. The staff information resource list (see chapter 1) may be particularly useful if it seems that the equipment or service is something that would be provided to the user directly—for example, finding community resources that provide funding for a personal aide, whose duties might include proxy borrowing privileges.

*Offer alternatives and encourage feedback.* If you need to deny a request, try to provide alternatives and ask for additional feedback. For example, if people request that your public library scan books for them but you do not have available staff hours, offer to provide a "tips and tricks" class on efficient scanning for individuals and their companions or ask if purchasing equipment such as CCTVs (see chapter 3) would address users' needs. Try to see this as an opportunity for participatory creativity, where both the librarian and the patron can focus on the ultimate goal and have a dialogue about the details of how this goal can be accomplished.

Accessibility awareness often persists: once you learn, for example, that there is an ADA Accessibility Guidelines regulation about wrapping exposed pipes under sinks, it can be hard to pass a public sink without checking it for compliance. More important, the ability to interact as naturally with patrons who have disabilities as with nondisabled patrons should also become part of library culture, both for individual libraries and for the field at large. Some ways to accomplish this may include the following:

- Recruiting and hiring more disabled librarians
- Ensuring inclusion in the library school curriculum
- Participating in continuing education
- Promoting a disability culture

## More Disabled Librarians

In 1998, Don Sager wrote, "There are no current reliable statistics on how many disabled persons are employed in the nation's libraries, and relatively few books and articles have been published on recruitment and accommodation of librarians and support staff with disabilities" (109). This does not seem to have changed significantly. The American Library Association does sponsor the Century Scholarship, an annual award for library students with disabilities (http://www.ala.org/ascla/asclaawards/asclacentury), and the LibraryCareers.org "Diversity in Libraries" page (http://librarycareers.drupalgardens. com/content/diversity-libraries) mentions people with disabilities but does not have an active link to resources.

This is unfortunate, since library careers might be a good choice for many people with disabilities. Accommodations for staff members with disabilities can be as easy as moving a file cabinet or setting up some of the built-in or open-source computer technologies mentioned in chapter 6. The Job Accommodation Network has a useful website of accommodation needs and solutions at http://askjan.org; it can also provide free consultation about situations not covered on the site. As Marie Bruni (1998, 110), former director of the Huntington (NY) library who has multiple sclerosis, has pointed out, "I know of no other profession where accommodations can so easily be made . . . and where there is such a variety of jobs to be performed, many of which are adaptable."

In addition, the field will benefit from librarians whose awareness of accessibility issues may be enhanced by their own experiences with disability. One clear opportunity is the potential for more initiatives, such as the Library for Deaf Action (http://folda.net), which was started by Alice L. Hagemeyer, a Deaf librarian, and which has been active for many years "to promote library access and quality library resources for the deaf community globally." The Library for Deaf Action publishes the Red Notebook, which includes posters and programming suggestions for attracting Deaf patrons; after the initial $25 purchase, all updates are provided at no charge. Its current president, Alec McFarlane, is working to establish a nationwide Deaf Cultural Digital Library system, modeled on the National Library Service for the Blind and Physically Handicapped; more information is available at http://connect.ala.org/node/156827.

## Inclusion in the Library School Curriculum

If students are aware of disability and accessibility topics as part of career training, they will have a range of knowledge that they can bring to their professional activities. There are currently single accessibility-related classes being introduced into the library curriculum; for example, Jacob Wobbrock taught a research seminar on accessibility at the University of Washington in the spring of 2012, and Joyojeet Pal started a popular course on assistive technology, including a cultural awareness component, at the University of Michigan in the fall of 2013. As the professional demand for cultural competency around working with patrons who have disabilities, elderly patrons, and so forth grows, the availability of such classes will likely increase.

## Continuing Education

Look for presentations and meetings about accessibility at library conferences. For example, the 2013 American Library Association conference had a presentation entitled "Different Strokes: Serving the Health Information Needs of a Diverse Community" and a meeting of the Universal Accessibility Interest Group, which was sponsored jointly by the Association of College and Research Libraries and the Library and Information Technology Association.

There are also a large number of online webinars on various accessibility topics; the resources listed here provide at least some webinars at no charge and may also keep archives of previous webinars:

*Accessibility Online:* webinars related to various aspects of legal compliance (http://www.accessibilityonline.org/Schedule).

*U.S. Access Board:* webinars related to various aspects of legal compliance (http://www.access-board.gov/webinars-calendar/cat_listevents).

*SSB BART:* webinars related to technology and accessibility (https://www.ssbbart-group.com/webinars.php).

*Project EASI:* webinars related to technology and accessibility (http://people.rit.edu/easi).

*AT Coalition:* webinars related to technology and accessibility (http://atcoalition.org/trainings).

*National Center on Accessible Instructional Materials:* webinars on materials accessibility, focused on the K–12 classroom but with implications elsewhere (http://aim.cast.org/experience/training/webinars).

Doing an online search for "free accessibility webinars" will likely bring up a useful list as well.

## Promotion of Disability Culture

While there has been considerable debate about whether disability can be considered a cultural attribute, there are definite disadvantages to seeing disability solely as a medical issue that requires accommodation. Matthew Ciszek (2012), in his article "Diversifying Diversity," talks about the need for including older students, LGBT (lesbian/gay/bisexual/trans) students, and students with disabilities in creating a multicultural library environment. Yet while article readers are encouraged to purchase books about parenting and support LGBT events, the only suggestions around disability are related to topics such as adjustable tables and alternative formats; there is no apparent awareness of the wealth of literature, media, and activism resources that people with disabilities have established.

Ways that your library can begin to promote disability culture include the following.

*Check with your accessibility resource people to get on mailing lists for local disability-related events.* Offer to use your standard library communication channels to publicize the event. Consider whether it would be appropriate for the library to participate in the event, such as staffing a booth. The library might even offer to host events or jointly sponsor events with local groups.

*Create a list of books and videos about disability-related topics to consider for acquisition.* One way to do this is to do an online search for "disability studies curricula" and see what materials come up more than once. You might also ask your accessibility resource people to suggest titles.

*Include people with disabilities in the library's promotional materials.* For example, show pictures of wheelchair users on your website on pages other than just the ones promoting your disability services.

*Brainstorm with your accessibility resource people about potential events and exhibits on disability-related themes.* Topics might include the history of the disability rights movement, noted authors with disabilities, or the evolution of disability portrayals in popular films.

## Key Points

Even libraries that have incorporated accessibility awareness into their culture cannot anticipate all patron needs. Specific accommodations may require some advocacy work with your administration or tact in letting patrons know that alternatives to their requests may be necessary. As more librarians become aware of how to successfully implement accessibility and as more people with disabilities enter the library field, this will ideally become an increasingly natural process.

In summary, the purpose of this book has been to encourage you to implement an ongoing consideration of accessibility throughout your library. Perhaps most important should be the willingness to go beyond standard guidelines and mandates to create an environment fully geared toward appreciation of people with disabilities as library patrons. After all, as someone once said, your library needs and wants to attract more patrons with disabilities.

## References

Bruni, Marie. 1998. "Disabilities Represent No Obstacles to Better Service." *Public Libraries* 37, no. 2: 110.

Ciszek, Matthew P. 2012. "Diversifying Diversity: Library Services for Underrepresented Groups." *College & Research Libraries News* 73, no. 9: 547–49. http://crln.acrl.org/content/73/9/547.full.

Fisher, Roger, and William Ury. 1981. *Getting to Yes.* New York: Penguin Books.

Herzog, Brian. 2012. "Reference Question of the Week—6/3/12." Swiss Army Librarian (blog). June 9. http://www.swissarmylibrarian.net/2012/06/09/reference-question-of-the-week-6312/.

Lewkowicz, Bonnie. 2013. "Cool Cat: Bonnie Lewkowicz." With a Little Moxie (blog). July 20. http://www.withalittlemoxie.com/blog/cool-cat-bonnie-lewkowicz/.

Sager, Don. 1998. "No Barriers to Service: Librarians with Disabilities." *Public Libraries* 37, no. 2: 109–10.

Schneider, Carl D. 2006. "What It Means to Be Sorry: The Power of Apology in Mediation." http://www.mediate.com/articles/schneiderc1.cfm.

## ◎ Resources

Accessibility Online webinars. http://www.accessibilityonline.org/Schedule/.

Association of College and Research Libraries. 2013. "The Power of Personal Persuasion: Advancing the Academic Library Agenda from the Front Lines." http://www.ala.org/acrl/sites/ala.org.acrl/files/content/issues/marketing/advocacy_toolkit.pdf.

AT Coalition webinars. http://atcoalition.org/trainings.

Job Accommodation Network. http://askjan.org.

Library for Deaf Action. http://folda.net.

National Center on Accessible Instructional Materials webinars. http://aim.cast.org/experience/training/webinars.

Project EASI webinars. http://people.rit.edu/easi/.

SSB BART webinars. https://www.ssbbartgroup.com/webinars.php.

U.S. Access Board webinars. http://www.access-board.gov/webinars-calendar/cat_listevents/.

# Appendix A: Questions for Accessibility Resource People

USE THIS FORM TO IDENTIFY THE QUESTIONS MOST RELEVANT to your library's needs and to check off when the question has been asked as part of a survey, focus group meeting, or other activity. Blank lines are left for you to fill in your own questions.

What Is Accessibility? (Chapter 1)

Can you tell us about people or organizations in the community that we should involve as additional accessibility resources?

Communication (Chapter 2)

What language conventions would you like the library to use to describe people with your type of disability?

For patrons with speech and/or cognitive disabilities: What items should we include on a communication board that we make available to patrons?

For Deaf patrons: What basic sign language vocabulary should library staff know?

For Deaf/hard-of-hearing patrons: What lip-reading/sign language alternatives would be useful—paper/pencil, typing on a computer, texting?

For Deaf/hard-of-hearing patrons: What are some good local resources for finding sign language interpreters, computer-assisted real-time translation providers, and other professionals who can assist with communication between Deaf and hearing people?

For Autistic patrons: Should the library provide interaction badges? How else can we help Autistic people use the library?

## Materials (Chapter 3)

For all patrons with print disabilities: What text formats are most accessible for you—e-books, large print books, Word files? Or do you prefer other formats, such as MP3s?

For patrons with low vision: If we buy a CCTV, what features would you like it to have? Are there any specific models you would recommend?

For blind patrons: Have you done any scanning of print materials into an electronic format? If so, did you use a screen reader with a mainstream OCR (optical character recognition) program or a specialized speech-output OCR program, such as OpenBook or Kurzweil 1000? What do you like or dislike about the methods that you have used?

For blind patrons: What are your braille access needs?

## Architecture and Environment (Chapter 4)

Is it easier to read signs that use black text on a white background, white on black, or some other color combination? Where should we place signage so it is easiest to read?

For patrons with environmental illness/multiple chemical sensitivity: What specific steps do you suggest to maximize the accessibility of our environment for your safety?

What other changes can we make to our environment to increase our accessibility?

Would you help us do a walk-through of the library to ensure that items are placed logically, that no barriers exist, and so on?

## Trainings and Events (Chapter 5)

Are there particular aspects of the event that you are concerned about being accessible? What are your suggestions on how to address these aspects?

What should we be sure to mention as a potential access issue in our publicity for the event?

## Technology (Chapter 6)

What assistive technology do you already use with your computer/mobile device? What do you like/dislike about it? Would you be willing to help the library provide support for its use if we acquire it?

## Web Accessibility (Chapter 7)

Would you be willing to help test and provide feedback on the accessibility of our website, as it currently is and as we design or redesign it?

## The Accessible Library (Chapter 8)

Would you be willing to provide letters or other indications of support for funding accessibility-related equipment or initiatives?

What other community resources provide accommodations to the public?

What are local disability-related events that we can participate in?

What types of programming (events, exhibits, etc.) can we provide around disability topics?

# Appendix B: Checklist for Presentation/ Lecture Accessibility

**Room booking**

Room is the closest available to accessible bathrooms.

Room has not been recently upgraded (new paint, new carpet, etc.).

**Room setup**

Aisles are at least 36 inches wide.

Sufficient turning space (at least 60-inch diameter) is provided for wheelchair users.

Space to approach and move away from handout tables is provided (see Americans with Disabilities Act specifications, p. 47).

Space to approach and move away from refreshment tables is provided (see Americans with Disabilities Act specifications, p. 47).

Move furniture away from windows or cover windows to avoid backlighting of sign or voice interpreters.

Ensure that presenters who cannot access the standard podium can access a small table and a handheld or lavaliere microphone.

Ensure that if there are multiple presenters, they are all seated at the same level (e.g., in front of the stage if the stage is not accessible).

## Staffing

Arrange for staff or volunteers to be available to help with wayfinding, getting food, and so on.

Arrange for interpreters, computer-assisted real-time translation, or other personnel who will be needed in response to automatic or requested accommodations.

Arrange for materials to be provided ahead of time and in alternative formats as requested.

## PowerPoint Design

Use simple fonts, not in all caps.

Type size: at least 72 point for headings and 48 point for body text.

Provide good font/background contrast; consider white text on a black background.

Left-align text, place graphics on the right.

Use numbered bullets.

No more than 7 lines per slide.

Use clear language.

Avoid "special effects."

## Before the Presentation Starts

Provide information about relief/break areas for people with service dogs.

Provide accessibility information (e.g., location of accessible bathrooms) during introduction.

## During the Presentation

Write as large as possible on easels, white boards, and so forth.

All speakers should use microphones.

Audience members should be given microphones when they speak, or presenters should repeat questions/comments.

# Appendix C: Test Plan for Hometownlibrary.com

THANK YOU FOR YOUR HELP WITH REVIEWING OUR NEW WEBSITE! If you have any questions, please contact Bunny Watson at 555-222-4447 or bwatson@hometownlibrary.com

| Task | Results |
| --- | --- |
| Find the address of the main library. | |
| Find directions on how to get to the library by public transit. | |
| If you wanted to contact the reference librarian to ask a question, what phone number would you call? | |
| What accessibility services does the library provide to people with disabilities? | |
| Does the library sponsor knitting classes? | |
| What hours is the Hartford branch open on Saturdays? | |
| Does the library own a copy of the book *No Pity*, by Joseph Shapiro? | |
| What is the library's policy on circulating electronic books? | |
| Find out how a teenager can apply for a library card. | |
| List one event that will be happening at the library within the next two weeks. | |

# Glossary

*accessibility resource people:* A term used throughout this book to indicate people in your community who can provide information and opinions related to successful implementation of your accessibility initiatives.

*American Sign Language:* A language that uses hand and body movements and facial expressions for communication. Its grammar is linguistically distinct from English.

*Americans with Disabilities Act (ADA):* Civil rights legislation passed in 1990 whose purpose is "(1) to provide a clear and comprehensive national mandate for the elimination of discrimination against individuals with disabilities; (2) to provide clear, strong, consistent, enforceable standards addressing discrimination against individuals with disabilities" (Department of Justice 2009).

*attention-deficit disorder and attention-deficit/hyperactivity disorder:* A type of developmental disability that can affect focus, organization, and impulse control.

*augmentative and alternative communication:* Use of devices to enhance or substitute for spoken communication. Options may range from a simple board where an individual chooses words or pictures to highly sophisticated electronic devices that can be preprogrammed with long speeches.

*autism spectrum disorders:* Developmental disabilities that can affect social interactions, verbal and nonverbal communication, and behavior. Asperger syndrome is a type where acquisition of language skills is less affected than it is with other forms.

*auxiliary aids and services:* Defined in the ADA as "(A) qualified interpreters or other effective methods of making aurally delivered materials available to individuals with hearing impairments; (B) qualified readers, taped texts, or other effective methods of making visually delivered materials available to individuals with visual impairments; (C) acquisition or modification of equipment or devices; and (D) other similar services and actions" (Department of Justice 2009).

*blindness:* Legally defined as having "best corrected visual acuity of 20/200 or less in the better eye; or a visual field limitation such that the widest diameter of the visual field, in the better eye, subtends an angle no greater than 20 degrees" (Lighthouse International 2013).

*cognitive disability:* A broad category of disability types that may affect comprehension, memory, problem-solving capabilities, or other cognitive functions. The phrase is sometimes used to refer specifically to disabilities that affect intelligence.

*cued speech:* A method of communication that uses hand symbols placed near the mouth to facilitate lip-reading.

*deafness/Deafness:* Inability to hear. Unlike blindness, there is no legal definition applied to deafness. Some people refer to Deafness as a cultural and linguistic identity, distinct from deafness as a medical condition.

*developmental disability:* A significant disability that an individual first experiences before age twenty-two and that is expected to last throughout one's life. The term is sometimes used specifically to refer to disabilities that affect cognition.

*dexterity disability:* A disability that affects an individual's ability to use his or her hands, caused by injury, amputation, or conditions that cause tremors, such as Parkinson's disease and cerebral palsy.

*environmental sensitivity or environmental illness:* Extreme reaction to chemicals, either natural or human made, causing headaches, breathing problems, digestive upset, fatigue, pain, or other symptoms.

*fair use:* The ability to legally use copyrighted materials for purposes such as creating a version in a format that is accessible to a person with a disability.

*fundamental alterations:* As defined by the ADA, a proposed modification "that is so significant that it alters the essential nature of the goods, services, facilities, privileges, advantages, or accommodations offered" (ADA.gov 2005).

*hard of hearing:* Reduced ability to hear. As with deafness, there is no legal definition that can identify when someone's auditory acuity can be classified as "hard of hearing."

*learning disability:* "A learning disability is a neurological condition that interferes with a person's ability to store, process, or produce information" (Learning Disabilities Association of America 2011). People with learning disabilities often have average or above-average intelligence.

*low vision:* "Low vision is a term that denotes a level of vision that is 20/70 or worse and cannot be fully corrected with conventional glasses. Unlike a person who is blind, a person with low vision has some useful sight. However, low vision usually interferes with the performance of daily activities, such as reading or driving" (Kellogg Eye Center 2013).

*obsessive-compulsive disorder:* "An anxiety disorder characterized by unreasonable thoughts and fears (obsessions) that lead you to do repetitive behaviors (compulsions)" (Mayo Clinic 2013).

*people-first language:* A linguistic convention that lists other salient facts about a person before mentioning his or her disability—for example, "lawyer with cerebral palsy," "grandmother with AIDS." It is currently embraced by some people and rejected by others.

*POUR principles:* The key concepts in web accessibility: perceivable, operable, understandable, and robust.

*print disability:* Inability to hold, read, and/or interpret printed materials, whether due to blindness/low vision, dexterity disability, or cognitive disability.

*reasonable modifications:* Mentioned in both Title II and Title III of the ADA as changes to "policies, practices, or procedures to avoid discrimination" based on disability (Department of Justice 1993a, 1993b). Changes that would result in fundamental alterations or undue burdens are not reasonable modifications.

*screen reader:* Software used by blind individuals to hear information spoken from the screen or to run refreshable braille output devices. True screen readers speak information that is not usually visible to sighted users, such as text descriptions underlying web page graphics; they also include many commands issued via keypresses or gestures that enable blind individuals to bypass use of mice and touch screens.

*Section 508:* Refers to the 1998 amendment to the Rehabilitation Act of 1973. Section 508 is best known for covering accessibility to websites, but it also applies to software applications that are not web based, telecommunications, multimedia, and some types of hardware. It primarily affects federal agencies, but parts of the law may affect other entities, such as organizations that receive federal funding.

*Signed Exact English:* A language that uses hand and body movements to communicate, with modifications to the vocabulary of American Sign Language and the same grammar as English.

*speech-to-speech:* A free, nationwide relay service that facilitates communication for people who have difficulty with hearing and/or speech.

*text-to-speech:* Software used by individuals with disabilities other than blindness to hear information spoken from the screen. Generally, text-to-speech programs only speak information that is also visible.

*undue burden:* As defined in the ADA, "significant difficulty or expense incurred by a covered entity, when considered in light of certain factors" in providing an accommodation (Job Accommodation Network 2013). Factors include the nature of the accommodation and the financial resources of both the entity and its parent organization.

*user agents:* As defined by Web Content Accessibility Guidelines 2.0, "any software that retrieves, renders and facilitates end user interaction with Web content, or whose user interface is implemented using Web technologies" (World Wide Web Consortium 2011). Common examples include browsers, media players, and assistive computer technologies.

*Voluntary Product Accessibility Template (VPAT):* A form that describes a product's compliance with Section 508 regulations.

*Web Content Accessibility Guidelines 2.0 (WCAG 2.0):* A widely adopted set of guidelines used to evaluate website accessibility. As of this writing, WCAG 2.0 compliance is not mandated, but compliance with guidelines similar to WCAG 2.0 level AA is likely to be legally required in the near future.

# References

ADA.gov. 2005. "Reaching Out to Customers with Disabilities. Lesson One: Policies, Practices, and Procedures." http://www.ada.gov/reachingout/lesson12.htm.

Department of Justice. 1993a. "The Americans with Disabilities Act Title II Technical Assistance Manual." http://www.ada.gov/taman2.html.

———. 1993b. "The Americans with Disabilities Act Title III Technical Assistance Manual." http://www.ada.gov/taman3.html.

———. 2009. "Americans with Disabilities Act of 1990, As Amended." http://www.ada.gov/pubs/adastatute08.htm.

Job Accommodation Network. 2013. "ADA Glossary of Terms." http://askjan.org/links/adaglossary.htm.

Kellogg Eye Center, University of Michigan. 2013. "Low Vision." http://www.kellogg.umich.edu/patientcare/conditions/lowvision.html.

Learning Disabilities Association of America. 2011. "Defining Learning Disabilities." http://www.ldaamerica.org/new_to_ld/defining.asp.

Lighthouse International. 2013. "Social Security Administration: Definition of Legal Blindness." http://www.lighthouse.org/about-low-vision-blindness/definition-legal-blindness/.

Mayo Clinic. 2013. "Obsessive-Compulsive Disorder: Definition." http://www.mayoclinic.com/health/obsessive-compulsive-disorder/DS00189

World Wide Web Consortium. 2011. "Definition of User Agent." http://www.w3.org/WAI/UA/work/wiki/Definition_of_User_Agent.

# Index

boomers (demographic contingent), 28, 47, 53, 89, 113. *See also* elders

braille, 30–32; refreshable braille, 78–79

captioning, 36–37, 52, 89–90, 98, 105

CART. *See* computer-assisted real-time translation

CCTV. *See* closed-circuit television

Chafee amendment, 26–27

checkout machines, accessibility of, xii–xiii

children, 21, 26, 31, 43, 45–47, 52, 66–68

Chrome browser, accessibility options, 78, 81

closed-circuit television (CCTV), 29–30

cognitive disabilities: accommodations, 26, 65, 68–69, 79, 82, 84–90, 100–101, 108; definition, 135

communication, 5–6, 13–24; attitudes of people with disabilities, 14; with augmentative and alternative communication users, 15; with austistic people, 5, 20–21; with blind people, 19–20; with deaf people, 18–19; general etiquette, 13, 15–16; language, 14–15; with hard-of-hearing people, 6, 18–19; language, 14–15; with people demonstrating unusual behavior, 21–22; with people who have speech disabilities, 6; with verbose people, 6

communication boards, 5, 17

computer-assisted real-time translation (CART), 19, 66

copyright law, 26–28, 30

cued speech, 19, 136

DAISY. *See* Digital Accessible Information System (DAISY)

deafness/deafness: accommodations, 13, 15, 36, 45, 69, 89–90, 122; communication and etiquette, 15, 18–19; definition, 136

Dewey Pictograms (Oakland Public Library), 17

developmental disability, definition, 136

dexterity disability: accommodations, 49, 66, 74, 83–88; definition, 136

Digital Accessible Information System (DAISY), 35

dining surfaces, 46

disability culture, 123–24

disability simulations, 9

display enhancement on monitors, 80–82

Docs (cloud-based word processor). *See* Google Docs

drinking fountains, 45

drop boxes, 47

Drupal (authoring software), 111

DVDs, 36

Dvorak layouts, 86

dyslexia. *See* learning disabilities

e-book readers, 8, 35, 78, 82. *See also* names of specific readers

e-text, 35–36

Ease of Access (Windows control panel), 75, 80, 83, 85, 90–91

elders, 53, 64, 68, 80. *See also* boomers

electromagnetic sensitivity. *See* environmental sensitivity or environmental illness

environment, accessibility of physical, 47–49, 50, 56, 57, 64

environmental sensitivity or environmental illness, 53–54, 57, 136

epilepsy, 103, 108

etiquette. *See* communication

event accessibility, 61–71; checklist, 131–32; events with outside sponsors, 69–70; off-site events, 62; real-time events, 66

exhibit accessibility, 65–66

eye gaze systems, 84, 87

facility checklist, 54

fair use, 8, 27–28, 30, 136. *See also* copyright law

fire alarms, 45

Firefox browser, accessibility options, 81

Flash (web scripting software), 112

focus groups, 3–4

fonts, legibility, 5–6

Free Library of Philadelphia, 35

fundamental alterations, 2, 7, 16, 136

funding strategies, 9, 10, 51, 74, 120

Global Public Inclusive Interface (GPII), 76

Google Docs (cloud-based word processor), 33, 82

Google Sites (cloud-based authoring software), 111

grabbers, 52

haptic feedback, 79

hard of hearing, accommodations, 64–65, 89–90, 136; communication and etiquette, 18–19

Hathi Trust, 27–28

HTML, 32, 104–5. *See also* web accessibility

interaction badges, 21

International Instrument/Treaty on Limitations and Exceptions for Visually Impaired Persons/Persons with Print Disabilities, 28

Internet Explorer browser, accessibility options, 81

iOS devices: accessibility solutions for, 35, 75–76, 78–79, 82, 84, 86, 90; as accessible alternative to e-readers, 35; Flash and iPhones, 112

# About the Author

**Jane Vincent** is currently the assistive technology manager for the University of Michigan, providing direct assistance to students, web accessibility evaluations, and other activities relevant to electronic accessibility and universal access. She has provided consultation to libraries on accessible technology acquisition and use, as well as evaluation of website accessibility for businesses and organizations. Jane has presented at conferences of the American Library Association, the Public Library Association, and the California Library Association, as well as at multiple conferences on assistive technology, aging, and usability. She is the author of *Implementing Cost-Effective Assistive Computer Technology* (2012), and her writings have been published in *Library Hi-Tech News*, *JASIS*, *Communication Disorders Quarterly*, *MacWorld*, and the blog Access on Main Street. Jane holds a master of arts in library science from the University of Michigan and a bachelor's degree from Lawrence University.

# DATE DUE